KnitLit

THE THIRD

Linda Roghaar and
Molly Wolf, editors

Knit Lit THE THIRD

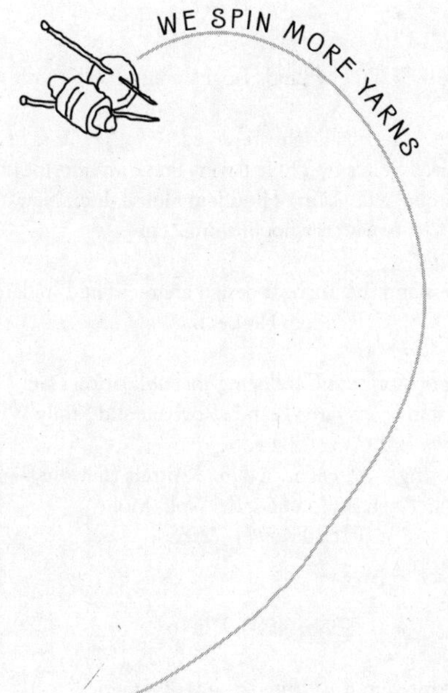

THREE RIVERS PRESS
NEW YORK

ALSO EDITED BY LINDA ROGHAAR AND MOLLY WOLF

KnitLit: Sweaters and Their Stories . . . and Other Writing About Knitting

KnitLit (too): Stories from Sheep to Shawl . . . and More Writing About Knitting

Published in the United States by Three Rivers Press, an imprint of the Crown Publishing Group, a division of Random House, Inc., New York.
www.crownpublishing.com

Three Rivers Press and the Tugboat design are registered trademarks of Random House, Inc.

Library of Congress Cataloging-in-Publication Data
KnitLit the third : we spin more yarns / Linda Roghaar and Molly Wolf, editors.—
1st ed.
1. Knitting. 2. Knitting—Miscellanea. 3. Knitters (Persons)—Miscellanea.
I. Roghaar, Linda. II. Wolf, Molly.
TT820.K6944 2005
746.43'2—dc22 2005008991

ISBN 1-4000-9760-6

Printed in the United States of America

DESIGN BY ELINA D. NUDELMAN
ILLUSTRATION BY NORA ROSANSKY

10 9 8 7 6 5 4 3 2

First Edition

FOR THE CHILDREN:

SARAH, HANNAH, ROSS, JOHN, GEORGIANA

Credits

A slightly different version of "Why Bother Knitting?" by Marjorie Flathers appeared in the July 2002 issue of *St. Anthony Messenger*. "How Knitting Saved My Life" © 2004 by Ann Hood was originally published in *Real Simple* magazine. A slightly different version of "Socks and Society" by Betty Jones was previously published in the monthly newsletter of the Peachtree Handspinners Guild, Atlanta, GA. "Knitting for Charity: An Awakening" by Candace Key was previously published in a slightly different form by Knitty.com in the fall of 2004. A slightly different version of "Baby Blues" by Adrienne Martini was previously published by Knitty.com. "Washing My Husband's Kilt Hose: A 32-Bar Reel" by Susan Blackwell Ramsey originally appeared in *Poetry Northwest*; reprinted by permission of the author. "In Which It Is Discovered That I Am Not Ann Patchett" © 2005 by Ann Shayne. "The Christmas Sweater" by Lauran Strait first appeared in a slightly different form in the e-zine *Gator Springs Gazette* in December, 2003. Reprinted with permission of the author. "A Knitting Circle" by Susan Gordon Lydon appeared in a slightly different form in the fall 2002 issue of *Interweave Knits*.

Acknowledgments

We are so fortunate to have a plethora of smart, competent interns who have helped with the painstaking task of compiling this volume. Special thanks to Rachel Engelson and Stephanie Meyers from the University of Massachusetts and Rachel Leach and Elana Kimbrell from Mount Holyoke College.

Sherry and Randall Brooks: thank you for your good work, beautiful colorways, and now, a way to find your yarn year-round, at www.brooksfarmyarn.com.

Thanks, too, to the sterling team at Three Rivers Press: Becky Cabaza, who shared our vision from the beginning; Carrie Thornton, who managed us so capably through *KnitLit* and *KnitLit (too)*; and now Katie McHugh, who has brought her fresh eye and editing skills to *KnitLit the Third.*

Finally, we want to thank Campbell Wharton for his enthusiasm and expertise in promoting the books. He became so involved with the books that he learned to knit, continuing the knitting tradition of his family. We appreciate his dedication.

Contents

PART TWO: *Who's in My Life*

By Blood Knit Together: Women

Expectantly: Our Young

Of Love and Loss and the Sweater Curse: Mates and Lovers

Knit Two Together: Friends

PART THREE: *What's in the Basket*

There Is Something Special About: Socks

Some Work, Some Don't: Projects

Loose Balls: Stash

Preface

LINDA'S STORY

My friend Margaret and I have planned to meet for a leisurely lunch, but a big yellow truck changes those plans. It all happens in the middle of the main intersection of Northampton. As she drives, Margaret's attention is somewhat distracted as she looks for a place to park. As for the truck driver—well, who knows what he is thinking? Obviously, he fails to see her green minivan, as he turns directly into it. One minute she is looking for a parking space, and the next minute all she can see is yellow truck.

Meanwhile, I'm sitting in the restaurant waiting for her. An hour passes. Where is she? A mysterious phone call to the restaurant seems not to be for me, but it includes the name "Margaret." My concern turns to worry. I call the local hospital. Has there been an accident? No, they say, but call back in a while. I have lunch, and try to take comfort in the food. I call the hospital again. Yes, there has indeed been an accident, but they have no details. Another half hour, I call again, by now on first-name terms with the receptionist in the ER. Finally, yes, they are bringing in a woman who had been in an accident in the middle of town. She is fiftyish—is that my friend? No, no, she's my age, not fiftyish. Oh, right. I am fiftyish. Damn. I take off for the hospital.

There she is, in a hospital gown in the ER, shaken, but whole. She takes one look at me and bursts into tears. Then it starts: the ER vigil. Wait. Ask two questions, submit to a brief test, wait. Wait. Wait. Wait for the next person who needs to check on you. Wait for the results of the test, wait to hear back from the insurance agent and the towing company who's made off with her van.

With dawning horror we realize our predicament:

WE HAVE NO KNITTING!

Margaret's knitting is in her van (which has been towed to some unknown location), and I have foolishly left home without mine. We begin to quiz the staff about the likely duration of her stay, not so much to find out when she'll actually get to leave, but whether I would have time to make an emergency run to Northampton Wools for yarn and needles to get us through the afternoon. The situation is deteriorating. I realize that I need to distract her, and quickly. She's not doing well, looking wan and shaky.

In desperation, I begin to do the next best thing to knitting: I talk about knitting. I talk about yarn colors. What might be a good color combination for the cover of *KnitLit the Third*? Margaret has a special gift for color. Not only does she dye her own quite spectacular palette of yarns, but she has a way of combining colors that makes for fabulous sweaters. She talks about color with passion. I want to see what she sees, but I seldom do.

Now, to distract her, I talk about how I had seen an amazing display of color at a booth at the Taos Wool Festival and again at Rhinebeck (the New York Sheep and Wool Festival), dyed by a woman with a remarkable color sense. Would those blues and greens work for the new cover? I struggle to describe the yarn, and the memory of the experience of discovering such wonderful colors and soft yarn helps me tell the story. She perks up. She begins to describe a yarn she, too, discovered at Rhinebeck, in shades of brown and gray. Before long we're playing a subtle game of oneupsmanship on who has seen the best yarn for the cover.

Nurses and doctors come and go. And we talk about the colors for the cover and always return to this fabulous yarn we had seen at the festivals—mine, blue, hers, natural sheep colors. Finally, we discover that we are both talking about yarn from the same farm: Brooks Farm in Lancaster, Texas, owned and run by Sherry and Randall Brooks. We babble about all the colorways Sherry has developed.

Suddenly, it seems, Margaret is told she can leave. We find the car (painful to look at), retrieve her knitting, and head home.

So this time it's not knitting that has helped pass the time and soothe us, it's the talk of yarn and color—specifically, Sherry Brooks's yarn. It seemed fitting that her yarn be part of the cover for *KnitLit the Third.* And so it is.

Pictured on the cover (left to right): Cabaret by Stacy Charles, Chapello by Gedifra, Relax by GGH, Primero by Brooks Farm Yarn, La Gran Mohair by Classic Elite, Siam by Trendsetter.

PART ONE

What's in My Head

OK, So Who's Normal, Anyway? Obsessions

Knitting Up a Storm

E. B. Clutter

Patsy Schubert has one. It's pink angora with tiny pink-and-white pompoms along the front edge and candy-striped ties and it looks terrific with her ponytail, especially when she's skating. I'm ten, a year younger than Patsy, and I wear a ponytail too and Friday nights I go to the rink too and I want one. I know I'm a clumsy skater, but maybe a very cool skate hat will help my performance. And if not, at least I'll look the part.

My mother, who can knit with her eyes shut or while watching TV or relaxing on the lawn and who's been knitting since she was six, listens as I describe my new heart's wish. "A headband," she says when I show her where it sits on the head and how it ties under the chin with strings. "Yes, it sounds quite simple if you want to make one." Not the answer I wanted. The answer I was hoping for was "Sure, sweetie, I'll make it for you this afternoon, while the cake is in the oven!" But I can see what's in her mind and she sees that I can see. "High time," she says with a half-smile. "You know Margaret's daughters all knit and so do Eva's and Sarah's," she adds, naming just a few of her sisters whose girls were all eager, as they were growing, to take up useful skills. Though I've always had these excellent examples before me, and though I am my mother's only girl, I'm not interested in learning anything that will take me off the playground or away from my beloved books.

"Look through my wools. I can start you today, if you like."

"Well, I do have to go to school, you know . . ."

She smiles as I frown. I know what she's thinking—one day of learning in her kitchen would do me much more good than a day in my grade-six classroom. She's keen on preparing me for running a household. It runs in her family. Her many relations pride themselves on marrying off their daughters while still in their teens. I have two cousins who each had a big engagement ring at sixteen and a huge wedding at seventeen. Now they're both overweight old ladies in their twenties and always yelling at their screaming kids. I have no intention of ever babysitting.

I have no intention of ever being anything like them. A decade later, when I'm in university, I will tell stories about these girls and laugh knowingly about the fifties. But not now. Now I'm ten. I love to write and I'm excellent in math. I've even skipped a grade and that's why I'm in the same class as Patsy. I find all housewifey things boring. But I do want a skate hat and though Patsy doesn't really talk to me, I know from what I've heard that Patsy's aunt made hers. My mom could so easily make one for me!

"Oh, look at the clock," my mother says. "You'll be late for school! Tell you what. When you get home, look through my wools. I may have a color you like, but if not we can pick up a couple of skeins when we're shopping this Saturday."

"We don't have to go downtown, do we?" I whine, but I'm already planning. "Okay, I want it two-tone, baby blue and white!" I say, grabbing up a slice of toast to finish on the way. "With pompoms!"

"Three skeins, then," calls my mother as I run out the door.

All that day I'm picturing me wearing my creation to the rink next time I go with my friends. "This really keeps my ears warm!" I'll say, or, "This keeps the hair out of my eyes!" and Patsy won't be the only one to look great on the ice. People will look at me too.

That's the smooth part. What happens over the next two weeks is not. From the trip downtown—a tiring day filled with chores—to the choice of wools and needles, to the size of pompoms and placement of stripes, all is discord and argument—the permanent storm that is me and Mom. Me and the needles don't get on well either as I knit and rip, knit and rip. I can't get the tension right, I miscount the stripe rows and my decrease section is a woozy patch. I manage to get five good pompoms but they're bigger than they should be and they hang limply rather than peek coyly over the edge. Mom hovers with her own needles, demonstrating and advising, but she won't do my work. "Those are your needles. You should never hand your needles to anyone."

Good advice. But my temper flares over and over. Just when I really want her help she refuses. I persevere, and in the end I have what I want. A finished hat. Sort of. I wear it anyway. I'm earlier to the rink than usual and none of my friends are there yet.

"What's that on your head?" is the first thing I hear, before I've even laced on my skates. It's from this new kid, Brian, hoping to make friends among the boys by jeering at a girl. Usually people ignore him. This time others take up the call, looking and pointing. Soon Patsy herself skates over and laughs openly. Right beside her, her best friend Arlene stares in a disbelieving way and says loudly, "She's trying to copy you!"

"Yeah, and she stinks at it!" someone else adds. And from David, who always asks me for math homework answers and I give them, I hear, "Those pompoms look like dog-doo." They all skate off in a bunch, leaving me on my own. I am mortified. I want to cringe and sulk, but my hat stays where it is. By the time my friends arrive, I have a stomachache and have to leave early.

But the next week at school, a few of my friends ask me how I made my hat. "Easy!" I say. "I'm gonna fix mine, so if you get needles and wool, I can show you!" Over the next few days five of us eat lunch quickly and knit secretly in an empty classroom and the next skate night we're all there, wearing our wonky hats, smiling and smirking to a high pitch. There's Patsy off to one side pretending to be special, and on the other side of the rink there's us, whooping it up and having a grand time. "This really keeps my ears warm," we call to each other, and "Yeah, it really keeps the hair off my face!"

By the end of winter, there isn't a girl in my class who doesn't have a skate hat and I feel responsible. Show-off Patsy, feeling much mocked, has stopped wearing hers. Poor kid. Not the sharpest crayon in the box and since she has nothing new to show us, no longer a style maven either. But that's the adult me recalling her. The ten-year-old me is overjoyed. A decade later in the sixties, when I'm in university and into taking action against social injustice, I will consider this to be my first big success.

But in the meantime there's a lot of heavy weather to ride. Things at home get pretty frosty as I hit sixteen and still I cling to my own ideas. Mom and I are constantly colliding. For one thing, I'm not interested in getting engaged and I insist on finishing high school. I know she's envious of her sisters' success with their daughters—all of them apparently great household managers. I know she wants me to be the same. And I'm not. I even veer from knit to crochet—it's the time of mod vests and caps after all, and I'm a girl of my time.

I imagine over the years she takes a verbal beating from her sisters for her wayward daughter. Perhaps she's been agreeing with them all along, hanging her head in shame for my lack of useful skills, having nothing of her own to add when the bragging turns to sons-in-law, babies, and new homes in the suburbs. "Emma's so different," I imagine them telling my mother politely to her face. But the one time it happens in front of me, Mom brings them all up short. "Different!?" she demands. "Do you mean not talented? My Emma can knit! And crochet! And she goes to university. Which of your daughters ever did that?"

In the stunned silence I feel the two of us knit, the way a broken bone knits. Mended. Storm ended. Not forever but for now. And later in life I award Mom more credit still. In at least one skill, she caught me and taught me when I was eager to learn. In teaching we call that readiness. In life it's called good timing.

Knitters Anonymous

Charmian Christie

My name is Charmian and I'm a knitoholic.

I used to convince myself I was just a social knitter—you know, exchanging fixes for dropped stitches, discussing which brands pill the worst, who has the best colors. But I've come to realize I've got a problem that's bigger than the sixty-eight skeins of wool stashed about the house, three boxes of patterns under the bed, twenty-six circular needles, and thirteen double-pointed needle sets, combined.

It's time to face facts. I'm a classic binge knitter.

I can go months without picking up a needle or even thinking about that Lagoon Blue skein of 100 percent virgin New Zealand lamb's wool tucked behind the bookcase. But when the stress of winter sets in, my fingers begin to itch and before I know it, I'm saying to myself, "Just a row or two." And for a few days, I'll be able to control it.

But two rows lead to four, four turn to eight, and soon I'm only working my day job to support my habit. Even if I can keep it to a skein a day, it's expensive. I'm into the good stuff—pure wool, silk blends. None of this watered-down acrylic or synthetic nylon nonsense.

Weekends are the toughest. Three skeins of pure virgin

wool can fly like nobody's business. I start Friday night and emerge Monday morning, bleary-eyed with aching fingers. I know it's bad when I start padding the bottom of the wool basket with toilet paper, hoping against hope no one will notice. But notice they do. A new sleeve or a finished button band is a dead giveaway. I confess, I've even worked on multiple projects to make life appear normal, but it always catches up with me. You can't hide three half-finished sweaters forever.

I haven't always been like this. I kept it together fairly well in high school. Sure, I tried a few rows, but I could take it or leave it. Then in university, away from the watchful eye of my parents, I began experimenting with monochrome stocking stitch and quickly moved up to Icelandic sweaters. To this day, Alafoss Lopi can make my head spin. Those ski sweaters called for three colors, but it was straight knitting and I thought I could handle it. Pretty soon, I found myself dabbling with Fair Isles and then—bam! I was into the hard stuff. Aran knits with cables so complex you'd stand a better chance untying the Gordian knot.

It's hardest during the festive season when my friends show me their Christmas patterns and hand me a ball of the latest yarn, expecting me to stroke a skein of Rowan as if it were nothing more than twisted thread. As I brush the wool against my cheek, I can almost taste the designer color—pistachio. Those who don't know my story give me gift certificates to The Yarn Barn or discount coupons. If only they knew the damage they're doing.

Winter's setting in. According to the *Farmer's Almanac* it's going to be a long, cold one too. But this year will be different. I've got clarity and perspective. I've got willpower.

I've got a 20 percent–off coupon.

A pair of thrum mittens for my niece, or a scarf, can't hurt. . . .

Don't Knit and Drive

Barbara Fornoff

WARNING: What you are about to read is evidence of poor judgment and wanton disregard for the laws of the road. Danger!

It was an evening like any other. I was headed to my office, where I would listen and problem solve with the clients who come to me for counseling. As a psychotherapist, I consider what I do to be a privilege. People trust me to hold their secrets safe, and in exchange I listen and provide feedback so they can make changes in their lives. It is exciting and interesting work. However, because I talk about problems for a living, I need the balance of producing creatively with my hands. I am an accomplished weaver, but since you can't take your loom with you, knitting has become my newest passion. And with my knitting by my side, any wait for a patient became a pleasure.

There was only one problem with my job—the traffic! What had once been a wonderful journey to my office had become a nightmare of traffic gridlock. My response to the gridlock had been to take the back roads, which were more pleasant.

This particular night, though, even the back roads were

packed. As I reached the only road I could take, I could see lots of cars ahead before we approached a traffic light. It was stop and go. My fingers drummed the steering wheel. My yarn lay in the passenger seat.

So I did the only thing I could do—I picked up my knitting needles and began to knit. I could get about two rows done (size 11 needless and thick yarn do wonders!) and then I'd crawl forward about three or four cars and then roll to a stop. Again, I picked up the needles and breathed deeply, reciting my new mantra . . . I am calm, I am knitting, I will not be stressed about this traffic that is making me late . . . repeat. And so it went, row upon row, until I found myself directly behind the cause of the traffic jam: a stalled car.

At that point I had two choices—ones you are probably all too familiar with. I could beg, wheedle, cajole, and plead with the drivers in the lane next to me: please, oh, please, let me in. I could see their angry faces and their refusal to let me get over because they were as frustrated as I was. Or I could just wing to my left across the double yellow lines and go around the stalled car in front of me, and be on my way. So, throwing caution to the wind, I went around the car, crossing the double yellow lines, and then came to a stop while I waited for the red light in front of me. I peacefully returned to my knitting.

Knock, knock, knock.

All at once, there was an angry tapping at my car window and a police officer staring at me, disturbing my reverie. I rolled my window down.

"Hey! What's with that?" the officer yelled, pointing back at the stalled car. I looked up at him, knitting needles in hand, and replied, "I'm sorry, Officer. Is there a problem?"

"You can't do that!" he barked back. "You can't cross the double yellow lines! That's illegal! I can write you a ticket!"

I (still clicking away) replied, "But, Officer, I had to get around that stalled car so I could get to work." This just made him angrier. "You can't cross the double yellow lines!" he fumed. All at once I realized, *Oh my god! I am, in my Zen zone, peacefully defending my scofflaw driving to a police officer! I am about to get a ticket for knitting!*

Snapped into reality, I hurled aside my knitting. As soon as the needles left my hands, I was back in my right mind. "Officer! I am so sorry! What I did was wrong. I apologize for my behavior." The officer glared back at me and yelled, "Okay, then!" Turning on his heel, he walked back to deal with the stalled car.

I understood then that my new nirvana, knitting as a way to cope with traffic, had to come to an end. I'll have to find another way to manage the stress of rush-hour driving.

Pity.

What's a Yarn Store Without a Yenta?

Sandra Hurtes

During a recent walk through Manhattan's Lower East Side, I was intent on visiting my old haunt from my knitting days, Sunray Yarn. Instead of finding a wonderfully tacky window display, where natural fibers and acrylics competed for space, I was met by a metal gate and a man standing nearby who said, "They've gone wholesale only."

In the days when I was a knitaholic, a stop at Sunray was as necessary as lunch at Ratner's in order to feel that I'd had the complete Lower East Side experience. Unlike the yarn stores on the Upper West and East Sides that catered to trendy and upscale knitters, Sunray was my way of getting real about knitting. Sure, I bumped shoulders with those who came there to purchase yarns at bargain prices so they could replicate the designers' latest, but mostly, Sunray was down-home yenta. Utica Avenue with a touch of Fifth. Sales people with names like Rose and Ida called me sweetheart while resizing a pattern in the time it took to say "Adrienne Vittadini."

In Crown Heights, where I grew up, I lived in an apartment building where the neighbors lived in each other's kitchens. "Don't talk to the yentas," my mother would tell me whenever she caught me spilling secrets, turning up her nose at what she considered their mindless chatter. Instead of getting friendly with the mah-jongg ladies for a weekly game, my mother got knitting by herself.

She created an endless array of garments for me and my brother, argyle sweaters that hung from her needles with bobbins swaying with each stitch, jackets with zippers and linings, and ponchos with braided fringes. Even with all the accessories these items required, I never sat on a misplaced needle or spotted hairs of angora floating in the air. My mother loved to knit. But she was neat and no nonsense. Instead of getting into the groove of hanging out in a yarn store, she'd make her selection and leave. No fondling, sniffing, or staring. And no yenta-ing.

Not like me. My mother taught my best friend and me to knit when we were eight years old. The two of us would sit on folding chairs in front of my apartment building, working our fingers, elbows, and mouths at a fevered pitch. Eventually other kids joined us working on lanyards and horse reins, and we formed a large semicircle of chairs. "Look at the little yentas," neighbors would say laughing as they watched us, their heads bobbing out of their windows.

When we left Crown Heights for a neighborhood where young and old didn't congregate outdoors, knitting became a more solitary activity. I'd sit under the hair dryer (those were pre-blower days) and create scarves for my father, brother, and boyfriend. Like my mother, I enjoyed being productive during downtime, but unlike her, I craved a network of knitters, not just to yenta with, but to be around those who appreciated the sloppiness of the sport. I wanted to knit with others like myself, who lost needles in sofa cushions and left trails of fiber wherever they sat.

In the early 1980s my fantasy came of age. Yarn stores popped up all over Manhattan, and "hand-knit" replaced "homemade" with its image of yesterday's grandmother. Leaving my office job with its sleek desk and steel gray file cabinets, I opted to make a living in a warm, fuzzy ambience surrounded by wool. Maneuvering my time between three part-time jobs, my passion quickly became my obsession. I formed a circle of friends from a subculture of women who loved—I mean lived—to knit.

Thinking I had found myself a cozy yenta-group, I hung out with my new knitting friends after work and on Sundays. Yet while the click of our needles reminded me of my childhood crafts klatch, the talk was strictly designer. Instead of discussing the lives of others, or even our own, we'd talk Calvin Klein. Demonstration of an intricate cable stitch would take up an entire evening's chat time, and on the subway ride home I'd take out my knitting and cleave to the warm looks of strangers.

Realizing that I wasn't going to find buddies to knit, purl, and kvetch with, I dug my heels into the profession and crossed the line into major-league knitting. Who needed a social life when there were so many sweaters to be created? My needles became an extension of my arms, and I never left home without them. And why would I? There were my three yarn-store jobs, and so much knitting to be done on the subway, at the movies (I used soundless plastic needles!), and even while waiting on line at the bank. It wasn't long before I couldn't stop.

I'd sit on the edge of my bed way past midnight and make up patterns on my needles, in the design-as-I-go method. While I went funky, my mother went Missoni. Like a one-woman factory, she produced them at record speed. The sales people at her local crafts store served her coffee and doughnuts while totaling up the register.

"I thought you hated the yentas," I said one afternoon, eyeing some powdered sugar on her lower lip.

"I never said I hate them," she replied, her eyes narrowing to small slits. "Just that I don't want to be one."

"If you're referring to me, I haven't yenta'd in years."

After my mother questioned my yenta quotient I found myself looking longingly at the customers who had "normal" jobs, trying to remember what it was like to go out to lunch. With bags of yarn scattered all over my apartment, nine to five, with its built-in boundaries, began to hold a renewed appeal.

Trading in my needles for a step on the corporate ladder, I regaled my new friends with stories about my knitting days. They'd tell me that they wished they had it in them to chuck it all for a chance at odd schedules, work they could do with their hands while talking at the same time.

I didn't tell them that I hadn't small-talked in years. Instead I made up for lost time, yakking it up with my new friends over lunch. But back at the office, I missed the smell of sweat and sheep and the feel of angora against my cheek.

I decided to compromise, spending my off-work time in search of the perfect knitting store. Walking around the Lower East Side one day, I wandered into Sunray for the first time. Quickly I got the lay of the land—bright lights, low prices, comfy sales people. Rose asked if she could help me. She taught me basket stitch while telling me about her granddaughter's bat mitvah. I then told her about the promising date I'd had the night before. A passerby leaned over to admire the English tweeds in charcoals and browns I'd gathered. My sweater pattern became a joint venture. Time passed so quickly, I couldn't wait for the next Sunday. And so began my love affair. After a week of work in a Manhattan skyscraper, I'd visit Sunray where I'd revel in the crescendo of voices and the click of needles, and return to the life of my inner yenta.

Like all good shoppers, I couldn't help but stock up on the chenilles, mohairs, and lanolin-based tweeds. For months of Sundays, I'd carry home filled-to-the-brim shopping bags, until these precious yarns tumbled from my closet.

Sadly, like so many other objects of my desire that become familiar, I grew fickle about Sunray. While diving through my leftover bins, I realized I could shop in my own closet.

Many years passed. Years in which I found my way to other crafts, other interests, other loves. But none of them fed me in the way knitting and Sunray had. I needed to return. I dressed warmly one Sunday morning and left home for a walk to the Lower East Side. Filled with equal parts nostalgia and anticipation, I couldn't wait to open the door to Sunray and whisper, "I'm home." But when I arrived, all that greeted me was shaded glass. I was so disappointed. Not only had I left my beloved store; Ida, the customers, the fabulous goods, they'd all left me.

There would be no more bags full of bargains. But worse than that, I'd miss the talk, the helpful customers butting in, the finagling, and most of all, the opportunity to set the yenta in me free.

Cast Off

Robin M. Allen

I never finish anything I start. Dozens of novels and short-story collections languish on wooden shelves, bookmarked where I left off reading. Two of my bedroom walls are painted Canyon Clay and the other two still glow Drywall White. And after two weeks of studying travel guides, wading through websites, and reviewing glossy brochures, my vacation plans to Quebec have yet to be finalized.

I blame it on knitting.

When I was in the fifth grade, my Spanish teacher taught me how to knit. My first project was a scarf, and I didn't finish it. I know this for certain because I found it recently—three-quarters of a red-and-green-acrylic homage to Christmas looped around fat white needles—abandoned in a cardboard box along with other knitting projects in various states of doneness.

Despite my halfhearted beginnings, I love everything about knitting—settling into a chair with a steaming mug of cinnamon coffee, feeling slick nylon ribbon or nubby silk between my fingers, hearing the soft click of wooden needles, repeating the Zen-like mantra of knit-and-purl. I lose myself in these soothing rituals.

But as much as I enjoy the ceremony of knitting, I hardly ever finish a sweater.

Toward the end of a project, I start looking ahead to the next one. And then I drive to the yarn shop. Just one little trip. Just to see if anything good is on sale. When I open the door to the store, the perfume of Egyptian cotton, chenille, and merino wool makes my knees weak. High on the fragrance of possibility, I'm lured down the narrow aisles by exotic imported yarns. I'm seduced by colors like Emerald Forest and Chic Bisque. Almost without realizing it, I have made my choice and produced my credit card. All sales final.

Home with my treasure, I slide my current project aside, and start flipping through books and magazines in search of a worthy pattern. A cabled pullover (pictured in icy blue cotton) is perfect for the Chocolate Truffle wool I brought home. As I read the list of materials, I absently wind the factory-coiled skeins into neat balls. Then I scout my hardware for the straight needles, cable needles, and stitch holders I'll need.

I know I should finish the current sweater. It's almost done. I need to finish the right sleeve, then block the pieces and sew them together. But the new one is fresh and uncomplicated. It hasn't gone astray because I read the pattern wrong and had to unravel twenty rows and erase twenty tick marks. The yarn isn't rubbing my index finger raw.

The new sweater shimmers with promise.

Before I know it, I've cast on 120 and begun the knit-two, purl-two of the ribbing, promising myself that I'll finish the other sweater later. I only want to see how the new yarn knits up. I switch to larger needles and in a few days, the back of the sweater is done.

Of course I never finished the sweater I set aside for the Chocolate Truffle pullover. I didn't finish that one either. It was preempted by a Chinese Ginger vest, which was in turn cast aside for a Bubblegum Pink V-neck. They're all resting with the Christmas scarf in a storage box under my bed, next to a crate of sewing projects. I'm going to finish them, too . . . as soon as I book my trip to Italy and finish painting my office.

Alter-Knit Winner

Amy Rosenstein

So, this is hell. Funny, how closely it resembles Mrs. B's chemistry class. Mica slumped even lower in her desk.

"Before you go," chirped the effervescent Mrs. Bluejay, "I'd like to mention the Make Your Own Fashion Show that's going on a month from this Friday at Point Mall."

The word "fashion" filtered through the bass-and-drum music pumping through Mica's mini earphones, and she pulled off one side, her interest piqued.

"Now, all my sewing girls will be participating—"

Ugh, not the MS. ITs—Martha Stewarts In Training. Mica

despised those girls. They were always in some sort of tizzy, whispering in the halls, their bubblegum-glazed lips pouting when their latest crush would pass by, or arguing with the gym teachers about the evils of blue-and-gold gym uniforms on spring- and fall-colored females.

"—but, the contest is open to the entire student body, anyone interested in creating an original design. We'll put on a fashion show, and the winner will receive a one-year scholarship to the Fashion and Design Institute downtown. The meeting's at three in the home-ec room!" Mrs. B shouted to the backs of the wholeheartedly uninterested departing class.

At 3:05 P.M., Mica closed the book she was reading in the last stall of the bathroom (the school library gave her the creeps) and made her way to the home-ec room, fashionably late. She tripped over a desk leg and fifteen blond heads swiveled, mouths slightly agape.

"My bad, Mrs. B. I'll just find a seat," she said, plopping herself down with gusto next to senior class treasurer and all-around prom-queen shoo-in, Mindy Shores. Mindy shifted her body and her entire desk, giving a dainty huff with the exertion.

"Pass it down, ladies." Pink sheets ruffled past with contest rules and project specifications.

"Well, if no one has any further questions, I suggest you get to work!" Mica was so deep in thought she didn't notice Mindy's perfect little painted toes tapping on the floor in front of her.

"You sew?" she asked, her eyes narrowing as if this would allow her to see inside Mica, to the core of her talents.

"Knit, but I definitely get the whole sewing thing. The machine does it all for you, right?"

"Look," Mindy snapped, "this isn't something you do on a whim. You have to be able to create a wearable piece of clothing. That scholarship's worth $15,000, so we'd all appreciate it if you wouldn't make a mockery of it."

"Don't worry, Mindy—my main goal in life is not to mess up yours," sneered Mica, getting up quickly and blazing past Mindy to the door.

Fueled by her encounter with the queen bee, Mica set to work that night on her design. She sketched out a cropped sweater, crumpled her sketch and tossed it on the floor. It was followed by a halter. Finally, she drew a long fitted sweater with elegant sleeves that flared slightly at the wrists. Perfect! Mica went into her bedroom closet to find the special blue-green yarn she had gotten for a steal last year. It was so soft and luxurious—she'd been saving it for just the right project. She wound her long brown hair up and pinned it with an orphaned needle, grabbed the bamboos she needed, and got started.

Four weeks of knitting until 2 A.M. had given Mica some very distinguishing under-eye circles, she thought wryly, washing her hands in the bathroom before lunch. Mindy appeared as if out of thin air. "All set for tonight?" she asked, baby blues batting. "Yep, all set," said Mica. "Thanks again for getting your friend to model for me." Mica had been shocked when Mindy had offered to help find a sweater model at the final meeting before show day last week, but she was grateful, even if the helper was of a questionable sort.

"See you tonight!" Mindy flounced out, but her voice, unusually high, remained, and Mica stuck her finger in her ear to quell the ringing.

Behind the scenes at the show was like something out of an

old movie where the heroine finds herself lost in the casbah—fabric, clothes, and people mixed at tornadic speeds, and it was hard to tell what language predominated. Mica searched frantically for Sara, her model, as her time on stage was nearing. Suddenly Sara was before her in the blue-green sweater, holding out its left sleeve.

"What happened?" Mica shrieked.

"There was this loose thread, and so I pulled it and the sleeve came off." Sara apparently didn't realize the impossibility of this tall tale. "So it's ruined." With that, Sara whipped the sweater off and tossed it to Mica.

Sputtering, Mica caught it. C'mon, think! She was not going to let Mindy's game ruin her chances. She ducked behind a screen, yanked off her clothes and donned the sweater, which, on her size 2 frame, made for a mini sweater dress. Stepping out, she spied a skinny red scarf. She wrapped it around her neck, pulled the sweater a bit off her shoulder, and made her way out onto the runway.

Swing your arms, stop, sexy pout, now back, swing, don't trip, look back, wink, run! Mica flew back to the safety of backstage, exalted and sweating from her first modeling foray.

"Too bad about the sweater," Mindy hissed as Mrs. B called for the designers out front. Deflated, Mica kicked an invisible bug on the floor with her army boot. One of the judges, a professor from the fashion school, spoke.

"We see a lot of designs every year, but we rarely see the kind of creative spark that we did tonight. We would like to congratulate Mica Giovanni for her unique design. See you in the fall!"

Mica shot a look at Mindy, whose pretty pout had puckered, and smiled a really big, uncool smile. Quickly regaining her composure, she said casually, "Sure thing."

License to Knit

Maria Jerinic

It was late in high school that I first watched James Bond work his wit and wits in *Live and Let Die,* and it was a year later, as a new college student, that I watched a senior knit and purl her way through an interminably long dorm council.

In both instances, I was hooked. I regularly perused the television and movie listings for Bond films, and after having my mother teach me the knitting basics, I carried my rows and rows of stockinette stitch with me to every movie night and contentious student meeting. (I didn't know what I was making; I just knew I couldn't stop.)

I used to think the only connection between my two obsessions was that they both allowed me to become the object of some genial teasing: weren't these interests incompatible with my Wellesley feminist agenda? Yes, I knew from the start that Bond (particularly Connery's) is a sexist pig, so while this dismissal of my passion for him was justified, such a reaction to my knitting always struck me as unfair.

Once I became a parent, however, I realized that these two interests, these two sides of me, really are—dare I say it?—knit together. When I was pregnant with my first child, I finally abandoned the afghan I had been working on intermittently for five years, and I began a hat for my baby. I finished it in two weeks. Then my son was born and so was a nice sweater, followed by a baby afghan, a baby girl, and another hat. And while I knitted, I watched Bond and mentally compared his incarnation as Moore to that of Dalton and Brosnan. I did this late at night, after both my children had finally succumbed to sleep for a few hours, and I was too anxious to do the same. My craving for this practice—Bond with knitting, knitting with Bond—only grew as my children did. And so, initially I attributed my heightened need to knit to my raging maternal instinct, and my ravenous appetite for Bond films to a desire to escape the mind-numbing drudgery of picking up superhero figurines one hundred times a day.

After all, Bond would never knit. Just try to imagine 007 armed with high-tech needles that allow him to break from his current project (perhaps a pullover for those nights spent relaxing on an island retreat with some new blonde) and dismantle the laser of a brilliant villain intent on world domination, all without dropping a stitch. Imagine him deciphering knitting instructions written in some secret code that normal people, like me and the owner of the local yarn store, can't figure out. Really, I can't see Bond berating himself for not knitting a gauge swatch or worrying about twisting his work on those circular needles.

And maybe that's the point.

It's difficult to imagine Bond worrying about anything. Bond is rarely frightened or remorseful, and when he is, he is always able to recover quickly and make a joke. He thinks on his feet, acting decisively and effectively. He has complete confidence in his course of action and never tortures himself for past decisions. He's always on, but he confronts each scenario with such aplomb. How does he do it? The martinis?

Imagine having such strength of mind. I am not, nor have ever been, a calm person, and I have spent many nights chasing sleep while I catalog my faults and mistakes. I don't need to face maniacal geniuses to get my adrenaline going. Electrical outlets, playground bullies, roaming dogs who target small children, and possible global destruction—they inhabit my nightmares. Fear is a constant, hovering on the edges of my consciousness. Will I be brave enough to protect my children from the threats this world holds?

Not only that, but am I cool and collected enough to conquer my own frustrations? Can I battle the surges of temper that threaten to flare up at the demands of stubborn preschoolers, and at my growing awareness that the professional life I worked so hard to create now resembles that unfinished afghan I abandoned some years ago?

I need what Bond has: that ability to face a crisis with a calm, reflective mind, with minimal self-doubt. My problems are considerably less dramatic and sexy than Bond's, but they are, at the least, equally challenging. The happiness and health of my children are at stake, and I have to outwit both the world and my own demons in order to complete my mission, which (by the way) can't be finished in two hours. It's a lifetime assignment.

And so I knit. I'm at it in the early morning before my children get up, during their naps, late at night. Whenever I feel particularly frustrated, I pick up those needles and stand over my children knitting and am thus unfazed by the pleading for soda before bed or popcorn for breakfast. Somehow the clicking of the needles, the feel of that yarn on my fingers, the satisfaction of watching a project develop, and the knowledge that I have developed the resolve to unravel, to start again when necessary, gives me the calm and the patience to face the dramas of the day.

So forget the spy. I hope my children will say, "It's the knitter who loved me."

Airport

Stephanie Pearl-McPhee

It takes a few minutes before I realize that the man with the gun has made up his mind. There is no point in trying to rescue the situation any longer. I think if it had just been the woman, it would have been possible to escape, but the man makes it out of the question. I glare at them both, wondering how much white-hot fury it's acceptable to show people who are armed.

I give them what they want and watch as all hope slips away. For years I've wondered what it would take to separate me from my knitting, and now I know. Semiautomatic weapons.

The thick-necked security officer watches me as I take my sock-in-progress out of my carry-on and shove it down the side of the suitcase I'm checking. I watch him as he puts the suitcase onto the conveyor belt that carries my knitting into the bowels of the airport. I stand there looking at the bag disappear and feel a mix of panic and anger. I'd bought wooden double-pointed needles just to avoid this moment. I'd stood in the yarn shop and held them in my hand thinking about how I don't even like wooden needles, but there was a slim chance that the metal ones that I'm partial to wouldn't be allowed on the flight. I'd bought these nonthreatening soft bamboo ones just to ensure that I wouldn't be separated from my knitting.

The security guard (I will resist the urge to call him a thug, since it seems like an overreaction when he's really just doing his job) doesn't seem sympathetic at all. He claims that my knitting needles make him "uncomfortable," and when I argue (rather strongly) that knitting needles are "allowed items" he reminds me that what is allowed on this flight is at his discretion. I contemplate showing him all the things that he is allowing me to carry that I could use for a weapon. My pencil, for example is sharper, longer, and more sturdy than the 2 mm needles he took. I want to point out that I could give someone a really wicked paper cut with my boarding pass and, if I were really inspired, a kung fu move with my purse. I stop just short of making all of these points when I realize that if I convince him of anything, it will only be that I might be a little too imaginative for this airline. A vision of me boarding the plane stripped of my belongings and clothing flashes through my mind's eye, and I retreat. This is a business trip, and the idea of explaining to my publisher that I have not arrived in Massachusetts because of an unreasonable "yarn incident" smartens me up.

I walk out of the security check into the waiting room and I feel empty and violated. I have . . . for the first time in years and years . . . no knitting.

The flight I am trying to get on is only an hour and a half long. It leaves in an hour. That's only two and a half hours without knitting. I know I can go that long. I sleep for longer than that each night. It's not like I'm so addicted to knitting that I'm getting up in the night to do a couple of rows to take the edge off. I can do it. It's totally reasonable.

But it becomes obvious in the first few minutes that yarn

deprivation is not going to go well. I experience immediate symptoms: irritability, restlessness, anxiety, and an overwhelming urge to offer to ride in the belly of the plane with my luggage. I pace. I look around. (I look for yarn.) I simply cannot remember what it is that you are supposed to do if you don't knit. Sit there? Just *sit* there?

People often tell me that I must be very patient to knit. They have no idea. Truth be told, I knit because I am the most impatient person in the world. I cannot sit nicely. I cannot wait. I talk too much and bother my fellow humans if I am not knitting. I knit while I read. I knit while I watch TV. I knit when I go to the movies, holding my knitting up to the screen so the light shines through the stitches when I need to see something.

I knit so much that it is a personality trait. Other people are cheerful, organized, or persistent. I am knitting. Without this defining quality, I'm left feeling like part of myself is stuffed into the zippered side pocket of my suitcase. I realize that the next two and a half hours are going to be about resistance.

The security team finishes checking my fellow travelers for contraband and stalks past me. I achieve my first act of resistance when I don't leap up and run after them with the express purpose of pointing out the irony of their actions. The joke is on them. I am more dangerous without my knitting than with it.

Sulking in my chair, I manage to endure the first thirty minutes of my sentence by thinking hostile thoughts. I invent scenarios in which the plane experiences an airborne emergency where the captain wails from the cockpit, "Oh no! The Blanketig-do-dad pin has snapped . . . If only a passenger had some sort of really long thin pointy stick to save us!" That would fix them. They would be sorry that they had taken my knitting away then. They would have to apologize to me and my pain would have changed the world of knitting forever. Well . . . if we survived the crash. I spend a further five minutes contemplating what it means, that I am willing to endure a plane crash to get even with the airline for stealing my needles.

This idea jars me enough that I start trying to get a grip on myself. I look around me. All of these people are not knitting . . . and not one of them looks like they are about to chew off the armrest of their chair or make hostile phone calls to the director of airline security. Some of them are just sitting. Some of them are working on laptops. (You could hit somebody over the head with a laptop and give them a nasty bonk. I don't suppose Mr. Security Guard thought of that hazard, did he?) Some of them are reading. It's been years since I read a book without knitting at the same time, but I decide to give it a shot. I wander to the airport bookstore and try to buy something, but they have no pattern books, no stitch guides . . . not even one skinny little knitting magazine. I buy four chocolate bars and eat them in rapid succession to help kill the disappointment.

I spend the remaining five minutes until my flight boards making a list of the things I am not knitting the security guard for Christmas. I continue this list (he is not getting mittens) as I walk down the hall (he is not getting a hat), down the stairs (a sweater is right out), and onto the tarmac toward the tiny little sixteen-seat plane. I briefly spot my suitcase as it is being loaded onto the plane. My feelings are mixed. Part of me feels better just seeing it and knowing that it is on the same plane as me; the other part of me is resisting the insane urge to beg the pilot for special permission to retrieve it. Since this is all about learning self-control, I get on the plane and begin counting down my time. Ninety minutes until I can be with my knitting. I only have to do ninety minutes. I've had babies. I can do anything for ninety minutes. The plane begins to taxi away. Eighty-nine minutes. The engine revs up . . . the plane picks up speed (eighty-six minutes) and abruptly . . . we stop.

An hour later I am back in the lounge as the shocking news sweeps over me. The urge to scream starts building as they explain that the still and silent plane I have been sitting in for sixty long non-knitting moments has had a "mechanical failure" (sadly, it is not one that can be fixed with the application of a long, pointy stick) and I will be delayed to the next flight. The silent scream threatens to become audible as the airline lady in her A-line skirt explains that this new flight leaves in four hours and that it doesn't go to Massachusetts, it goes to Connecticut, but that they are sorry for the inconvenience. Someone will be at the "help desk" in a few hours to help us with any problems this may cause.

When the lady finishes her little speech, the horror of what is happening sinks in. I am not going to meet the car my publisher is sending for me. I don't have a hotel room. The new plane is going to land in Connecticut (wherever that is) and I am going to have no idea where I am. I am almost hysterical. The gravity of the situation is beginning to frighten me and I start to wonder if I have a physical addiction to knitting and this is withdrawal.

The next several hours are a blur. I know that my attempts to cope with the few hours until the help desk opens are punctuated by several phone calls of increasing hostility to my agent. In my defense, I was alone, worried, yarnless, and unsure of American geography with only her phone number and a poor attitude. I remember trying to knit strips of the newspaper with my pen and pencil (this, by the way, is a completely lame idea and does nothing to help). I feel certain that I owe an apology to the passenger next to me in the airport bar who now knows more about turning the heel of a sock than is really reasonable. I reach my publisher and figure out where Connecticut is. It is really close to Massachusetts. I splash my face with cold water and buy chocolate. The moments tick by. I plan a handknit Medic Alert bracelet for yarn junkies and write desperately bitter letters to the president of the airline and the governor of Connecticut. I'm not sure what I felt was her fault . . . it was a difficult time.

When the help desk opens, Miss A-line is back. As I approach her I realize that I must try to look normal. I use a moment to smooth my wild hair a little. I take a deep breath and remind myself to speak slowly and calmly. Instead of tackling her around the knees, I gently touch her elbow. "Excuse me, Miss?" She turns and looks at me quizzically. "I'm so sorry to trouble you, I know you are busy, but I just need a little help solving a problem having to do with the change of plans." Miss A-line smiles her super-white airline smile. She knows how to do this. She solves problems related to delays every day. She looks concerned. I can tell that she understands that I have a genuine problem. Encouraged by her warm demeanor, I have a good feeling about Miss A-line. I feel reassured by her competency.

The look on her face when I request her help in retrieving my knitting is something that I will never forget.

"I'm sorry," Miss A-line says, beginning to back away from me a little. "Your knitting?"

"Yes," I say, resisting the urge to advance on her as she begins to walk backwards. I explain about the waiting, and the security guy, and how far Connecticut was. I explain that I am upset and that I would be willing to help unload the plane and that I really only need it back for a little while and that I wouldn't take it on the plane . . . just knit a little in the lounge, then they could put it back where it couldn't hurt anyone (though they should definitely consider the hypocrisy of allowing pencils and pens, which are also pointy sticks). I request an address to which I could launch my formal appeal. I provide her with a written description of my suitcase and talk briefly about the risks of hoarding luggage from people who might really need something while they were waiting, like medication or money or wool. I laugh a little (so she wouldn't think I was nuts) and smile at her. I'm sure she understands.

"I'll look into that," says Miss A-line. "Please—wait here."

I wait until they board my flight, but she never comes back.

Stinking liar. I bet she crochets.

We Learn, We Teach, We Change: Growing

Why Bother Knitting?

Marjorie Flathers

You're quiet as you get out of bed. You're trying not to wake Walt, even though he can sleep through a California earthquake, and has done so. You, however, are different. You've always been a light sleeper, and after more than thirty-five years of marriage, you recognize all his sighs and movements throughout the night.

But for you, any sleep, light or heavy, is impossible tonight. So you slip through the dark and settle into your favorite tapestry chair in the living room. You don't usually sit in the dark in the middle of the night, but nothing's been usual lately. You're feeling disconnected somehow, but it's not because your mother's funeral was a few days ago. You let her go years ago when dementia erased her mind and left just a shell surrounding emptiness. Something else is gnawing at you, and you're not sure what it is.

Your knitting bag sits in the corner, so you decide to work on the sweater you're making for Caitlyn. When you learned to knit as a child, you immediately fell in love with the feel of yarn gliding through your fingers. Soon you could move the stitches along without looking. Now the rhythmic knit-one-purl-two begins to soothe the tensions you've been dragging around, and your mind drifts back in time.

Too young for the jitterbug but not quite a baby boomer, you came of age in the 1950s, with Elvis and the early days of rock and roll but also with Frank Sinatra and the big bands. A time when things seemed easier and, somehow, better. You remember being allowed to knit during study hall in high school. You smile as you remember the group of seventeen-year-olds sitting in the stands at a basketball game calling out, "Knit one, purl two, Mr. Thompson, yoo-hoo!" and embarrassing the new young teacher walking along the edge of the court. That was as close as you ever came to misbehaving.

The images fly by quickly. Assorted jobs, marriage, three daughters, Cindy, Carolyn, Caitlyn, none of them interested in knitting.

"It's nice, Mom," they said, "but what difference does it make when you can buy a sweater already made?"

You tried to explain your attachment to knitting, but you couldn't find the answer, so you gave up trying. Even so, you kept on knitting for all three girls.

The problem is that you haven't any answers lately, especially to the biggest question of all: What happened? To the world, to your life, to yourself? You certainly never thought you'd get old. Of course, you knew the years would go by, but you assumed that if a person, especially you, did all the right things, kept your weight down, your appearance up, and stayed busy, you wouldn't end up with a permanent case of the blues.

You have everything you ever wanted: a caring husband and family, a comfortable home, lots of friends. So why do you feel so spiritless, so drained? Why don't you have the energy the women in the vitamin ads have?

You think about your neighbor, Linda, who acts like a left-over flower child. She, at least, always jumped into whatever came her way with both feet. "College was the best of times" is Linda's mantra. "There were drugs and such, of course, but what I remember most are the jokes and schemes we dreamed up. Oh, Judy, one time we even drove the dean's new Volkswagen into the science building and left it in the hallway. What a hoot! He never did figure out who did it." When Linda tells you stories, you smile weakly and say nothing.

"I should have taken more risks," you murmur to yourself now. Some teens back then were daring, reaching out to life, but not you. You were always so timid, so obedient, trying so hard to please.

Walt was never a demanding husband, but you tried to figure out where you might not measure up anyway and you fretted about that. Everywhere you went, there were doctors and dentists, teachers and pastors, friends and acquaintances, all waiting to criticize, or so you believed. And, in the background, was your mother's voice, questioning everything.

"You're letting Carolyn go to a sleepover at her age?" she'd ask. Or "Why do you volunteer so much at the girls' school,

Judy? You should relax more." Or "Do you really like that style of furniture, that kind of food, that shade of sweater?"

It never occurred to you to answer, "Because I want to" or "Yes, I like it a lot." Instead, you searched your brain for words that were acceptable, hoping to get the nurturing you needed. At last, you realized your mother couldn't give what you wanted, simply didn't have it to give. But you didn't understand why.

Now, in the middle of a stitch, you throw the knitting on the floor. As your girls say, "Why bother?"

For as long as you can remember, everybody seemed to belong to a special club, a club you could join only by being what you thought they wanted you to be. But along the way you stifled every real feeling, every true need, until you no longer had a clue what those feelings and needs were. You think of all the times you left the house determined to have the exact stylish look, say the right thing, appear perfect, and you still came home with the uneasy feeling you hadn't passed the test. You remember, too, the times friends let you down with a word or action that wasn't what you'd expected. You tried so hard to be perfect; "why couldn't they?" you often asked yourself.

The first glimpse of dawn slips in between the drapes, and you walk to the window. You hear the birds in the trees squabbling over some injustice, something probably as trivial as the things you've wasted energy on. But as you're about to turn away, one bird, so colorful that it's visible through the morning mist, breaks away and soars to a higher branch, and there, as a small ray of sun breaks through, it begins its morning song.

Other faces and places create changing images in your mind. You can't help grinning when you think of that spur-of-the-moment party at Walt's cousin's house years ago. You didn't have time to worry about clothes or hair or attitude. You just went and had fun. You remember the day when Linda tried to talk you into becoming a vegetarian and you surprised yourself by arguing with her, not giving in—and still remaining friends.

A voice from deep inside sneaks up and asks: What if you don't need to please everybody? What if others' opinions and comments don't matter all that much? What if you don't have to understand your mother? What if you can forgive her for trying to fill her life with yours instead of giving you what you needed?

And what if—wild thought that it is!—you can forgive yourself for not being perfect? Imagine all these things and then imagine singing your song. Can you discover what that song is?

You turn from the window and pick up your knitting. You smooth your hand over the intricate patterns as if you're seeing it for the first time. You knit a few more rows.

This sweater is for you.

Translation

Deborah Robson

After a good night's sleep, the dreaming path to consciousness floats through vermilion merino, jade-colored silk, chocolate qiviut, and sunny cotton, not yet spun into yarn: the pure potential of color and fiber.

I pick up a pad of white paper, each sheet crossed in both directions by pale-blue lines. I pencil Xs and Os and ⧅s into the boxes made by the lines, charting a pattern that will combine color and texture when translated into fiber.

I unroll a scroll-like needle case and lift a pair of knitting needles from its felt sheath. Sliding the tail of a ball of yarn through my fingers, I begin to transform the flat, colorless diagram into what I envision as a three-dimensional, short-sleeved, U-necked sweater in shades of forest green, black, summer-lake-aqua, and ecru, with a touch of white.

By the time I finish it, this sweater will have changed from my original concept. Developed through trial and error, it will become an extension of my spirit that will wrap around my body on its journey into the wider world. My soul will be protected, stitch by stitch, in cloth of my own making.

When I flick the plastic switch, power races to the computer monitor, buzzing the room with an artificial glow. With a few taps of a stylus on a touchpad—the computer equivalent of an excellent pair of needles—I enter the universe of an electronic document that will ultimately correspond with a roll of paper in a printing plant a thousand miles away, which will turn my CD of files into a knitting book.

As I establish master pages that control the placement of margins and page numbers; as I set type; as I select the titles and subtitles, the body text, and the captions and assign to them codes that will determine how they appear in print; as I place the drawings; as I do all these things, measuring in printerly increments of points and picas, I imagine myself as a new knitter, attempting to decode the mysteries of yarn and needles. I think, "What did I not understand then? What do

I not understand now?" and these questions guide my decisions about how to design each page.

After printing the tentative pages on standard white office paper, I pinch them together, holding them in pretend-book form, and envision the crisp black type and the hand-inked drawings on heavier, warmer-colored paper. I imagine another knitter having an easier time discovering creative freedom than I did because of the work I do now.

I long to pick up my needles and make real the color and texture and softness and drape implied by these symbols, to knit an endless flow of sweaters and blankets and hats and socks and mittens and shawls that could protect every being on the planet.

Through a twist of fate, I have become the book's publisher as well as its editor and designer. This change demands that I learn even more skills. Although I do not like bookkeeping, I love fairness and I want this work to continue, growing into a culture- and time-spanning safe-zone of knitting.

So I print out reports that summarize sales and returns and shipments and damaged books under headings like GROSS and NET and MNRT and QAV and BKO, and I pick up a magnifying glass so I can read the figures and I labor to understand their meaning and to determine how this information can help me ferry a small portion of human wisdom to a sheltered future.

It's like reading tea leaves, although more abstract.

Over ten months' time—until my eyes blur; then rest; then again—I put numbers into software that should produce correct invoices, inventory counts, and royalty reports. Repeatedly I punch a button; notice, track, and correct one error; then discover the next.

Finally, I push the onscreen button that says "calculate" and receive an accurate royalty report.

And so I am able to write the checks, including a small one to myself, and I relax briefly, knowing that for a little while longer the knitters who have written these books can continue to share their insights with other knitters, insights specifically meant to let us help each other break trail and keep the old pathways from being overgrown.

And so I restore my energy by casting 180 stitches onto a 3-mm needle and joining the stitches into a circle. I'm tired. Knit one, purl one is a good edge treatment for the fatigued. I form the two types of stitches alternately, my fingers fluent in the knitter's binary code. Between stitches, I flip the working strand between the needle tips, front-to-back for knit, back-to-front for purl.

Knitting in an idiosyncratic way probably learned from my grandmother, I throw the yarn with my right hand. For two-color work, I throw one color and pick the other. My knitting has been described as "inefficient, but incredibly productive." I think of it as a canoe or sailboat, rather than a yacht.

After years of practice, I can construct this now-restful ribbing pattern while half-asleep. Yet I recall how hard it was at first to form a single stitch. I sat at my grandmother's left side, both of us settled on the smooth, ivory-colored fabric of the loveseat. It was late spring. My feet did not quite reach the floor, and her voice guided my fingers. Learning to *knit one* probably felt as hard as the inventory and royalty and invoice-calculation software has been, as hard as figuring out how to ship large quantities of books from one place to another was last year, as hard as the page-layout software was two summers ago.

Ribbing flows easily through my fingers, growing steadily, reassuringly. Preparing electronic files for the printer is never easy, but I have a checklist to be sure I don't forget an essential task. The driver of the freight truck has taught me how to stack a shipping pallet and to encase the cartons of books in heavy-duty plastic wrap, binding them so they'll travel safely to a distant warehouse. From there they will be shipped, one at a time, to other knitters. Each of those people will, I imagine, open a book's covers and release the gentle aroma of ink and paper, select a technique or design, pick up needles and yarn, and, one movement at a time, replicate the actions, just as I did when I tested the book, sitting in front of my computer with a ball of creamy cotton yarn and my grandmother's size 4 plastic needles.

Perhaps we both imagine, as our paths invisibly cross and each of us makes these skills our own, the way our creative spirits can knit the world into solace and connection, one reaching hand and one experimental stitch at a time. We share the courage to try something new, to approach a skill that we aren't sure we can master.

A hand guides the tip of a knitting needle through a loop of yarn. Fingers, touching each other lightly, wrap a strand of yarn around the needle's tip, and a hand—slowly, surely—pulls through a new loop.

In shape and in function, this bent strand replicates every knitted loop that has come before or will ever follow. But from this one new loop, delicately tensioned between dream and reality, between one knitter and another, hangs a world of hope and learning, caught by both its ends.

Eighty-two Rows in Garter Stitch

Dorothy North

She has chosen a heavily slubbed skein of wool,
ionic pink and orange with purple flecks

that makes me wonder what she thinks she'll wear
it with. But that's her problem. Mine is trying

to find some common thread with this young thing
I've hired as my associate; since we work

together sixty hours a week, it might help
to carry on a conversation, have some social

intercourse outside of law, and since I don't
watch sitcoms and she doesn't read, and since

she admired the scarf I knit, I've offered to teach her.
Two basic stitches, knit and purl, though

the whole craft is called knitting. How we combine
the knits and purls is what makes the pattern.

Yes, it is a lot like computers, though much
more reliable and less frustrating. You almost

never have to upgrade in knitting. When you knit
on the knits and purl on the purls, every other row,

you get stockinette stitch, regular knitting.
Garter stitch is good to start. Just knitting

every row. No purls. Each two rows
form one ridge that looks the same on front

and back. To get you started I'll cast on
and knit the first row, which tends to be stiff. At the end

I'll show how to bind off. The rest is up to you.
Thirty years old, her hands tremble in a way a
six-year-old's

do not, though the fumbled mess is just the same.
This is so confusing. I'll never get it. What's the trick?

Geological sadness opens on me. I try to choose
my words
with care. *There are women, as we speak, with fifth-grade*

educations in the Azores, who are knitting right now.
She stiffens. I have been too pointed, as usual. I should be

more tolerant; I was a new lawyer once,
and useless. But at her age at least I could knit.

She says, *It doesn't have anything to do with education.*
My point exactly. Sit still and keep going.

On the other hand, it might be easier to use them
up and cast them off, the way the big

firms do, and skip this ruse entirely.
Try this, the rhyme I learned when I began:

In through the front door,
Run around the back,
Out through the window
And up pops Jack.

Who did teach me to knit at six or seven?
Someone now dead, for sure. My eldest sister,

pregnant with her own child, or my aunt, who we thought
was our grandmother because she raised our mother

after their mother died? My turn next
to twist the woolly loops in coded sense.

We stop to take stock. Sixteen stitches where we
started out with fifteen. An unintended

increase. She's pulling the yarn too tight when she runs
around the back, as though she wants to tighten

a noose around Jack's neck, and as a consequence
her stitches are tight and wadded with sweat. I can't talk

to her about boyfriends, either, though I've heard
she's had lots. Thirty and not even thinking

about marriage. No hurry, she says. I knit
English style but wish I knew continental.

I asked the old woman who owned a sad
little knitting shop in a concrete tilt-up

in the back of a run-down strip
mall if it was too late to switch. *How*

long did it take you to gain the speed
you're at now? she asked. *Twenty years*

or so, I guessed. *Well, do you have twenty*
years to get up to speed in continental?

How could she be thirty and not know how
to knit? All of us knew how to knit or crochet.

It was expected. Not much else was, though.
It took fire and tears to break out. Now, this girl,

hair helmeted in place like the Barbie her radical
feminist mother wouldn't allow, expects to

succeed. So I guess this is better. Her fuchsia nails
tick on the needles, gels, we used to call fake,

that she has to get done weekly by the
Vietnamese woman down the street.

Three inches pile up quickly in heavy wool.
Next step: stop to admire the work we've done.

Sunset. Pink and orange with purple flecks
that anyone admires. My hands. Your hands.

Drop Stitch

Jane McDermott

"Firemen do this," Camilla told us. "And sailors."

This comment was for Peter's benefit, to give him ammunition to counter any "only sissy boys knit" assault he might experience.

Peter looked at me long and deliberately and I understood that if he did find himself fending off such an attack, it would be because someone had let it slip that he had been knitting and the only person who could do that would be me, and I would die.

"It really should be called 'knotting'," Camilla went on, "because what you are actually doing is loosely knotting the yarn together."

It was August and the summer had become long for Peter and me. Camilla, our neighbor, had offered to teach us to knit for reasons I don't remember. What we created as the result of those sessions could hardly be called knitting. We each looped together a scraggly web of yarn that drooped off the needles into something that looked vaguely like insect nests. I was nine and this would be the last summer that Peter, who was eleven, and I would play together. Neither of us knew that at the time; what we both knew then was that days went on forever, time simply would not end. We never got older.

We never changed. Nothing happened in the place where we lived.

Camilla, who was well into her sixties, lived in the quasi-legal apartment adjoining Peter's parents' house. Her apartment was a showcase for her handiwork. A bride doll in an Irish knit gown graced a spare roll of toilet paper. The Infant of Prague wore an elaborately crocheted dress. Knit and fringed placemats sat at the table. Cozies and covers hugged all the counter appliances. Poodle dogs with floppy ears protected liquor bottles. Her furniture featured doilies and antimacassars. There were afghans and throws of every description, pom-poms and tassels from every lampshade, every drape, every door handle, the bedpost. Neatly labeled boxes in her closet held tassels to dangle from the lacings of your ice skates or to be used as key fobs. They were attached to the letter opener and the key to her desk. And there were boxes of booties. Christmas booties. Baby booties. Booties for watching TV. After-sledding booties. Booties for bed.

To my way of thinking, Camilla was the anti-Mom. She had never married; she lived alone. She drove a two-tone Rambler with a push-button transmission. Behind the counter at the pharmacy where she worked, she used a hypodermic needle to inject vodka into oranges for her lunch. She wore high heels every day and sweater sets—lots and lots of sweater sets—that she knit herself. All were exquisitely detailed; some had appliquéd flowers or fancy buttons. She wore them year round, heading off to work in the Rambler, puffing a Lark, and wearing a summer pastel sleeveless cotton knit while our mothers did housework in shifts or pedal pushers.

Our mothers appeared squat and lumpy beside her trim, stylish figure, which was probably due more to the staples of her diet—vodka, coffee, and cigarettes—rather than a regimen of exercise and sensible eating. She attended Mass every week like the rest of us, and although I never noticed her Communion-taking habits, our mothers did. Still, our mothers would gather at Camilla's apartment to watch *Peyton Place* like girlfriends. Neither of the husbands was ever home and Camilla didn't have one. The three of them delighted in the sinfulness of that fictitious town and would sit on the front porch of Peter's mother's house, talking about the program by the glow of their cigarettes late into the night.

Peter's mother approved of the time he and I spent together; my mother did not. She continued to hope that I would become interested in "girl things." Therefore, the knitting lessons were a pleasant surprise for her. Usually, she was horrified to learn of most of the activities Peter and I engaged in.

Camilla also taught Peter's mildly retarded sister Cathy to knit that summer. Cathy took to the task enthusiastically, spending the rest of the summer and part of the fall completing an ambitious tangerine-colored, three-quarter-sleeved angora pullover. I thought it was hideous, but even at nine I could tell she had done a good job. Peter and I graduated to creations that could generously be called scarves before we ran out of yarn, interest, and summer.

Summer gave way to fall, and as fall was becoming winter, Camilla offered a huge surprise to us who lived in this place, where everyone believed they knew everything about everybody else: Camilla revealed that the woman she referred to as her niece was actually her daughter. Camilla's niece's children were actually her grandchildren. And out of the blue, a man, a widower, appeared on the scene to marry Camilla. He was actually the father of this niece-daughter, the grandfather of this niece-daughter's children.

Camilla was eighteen when this niece-daughter was born; the father of this child was bound for college and a successful career. So Camilla told the world that this child was her niece and raised the child with her own mother, who agreed to call the child her own.

"People did things like that back in those days," my mother told me. "Like what?" I wondered, confused, but somehow knew better than to ask.

Camilla and her new husband moved to Florida where I wonder if she continued to knit sweater sets and booties. I bet she didn't. It's warm down there and she probably had lots of other things to do. She didn't live too much longer after that.

The rest of us got older.

Cathy collects shopping carts in the parking lot of a supermarket in the place where we grew up. She's in her fifties now and lives in Camilla's old apartment while her elderly mother lives in the big attached house alone. I don't think Cathy knits; I think she watches TV.

Peter and his cousin Arthur run a bar.

I moved away a long time ago and live my life in the open, thousands of miles from there. I knit a sweater once, with gray and black tweedy yarn and a lot of determination. It's still worn by the person I gave it to.

The only knitting I do now is stories like this one.

Knitting for Charity: An Awakening

Candace Key

I have been a serious knitter since the early 1980s, when a friend cleverly bribed me into learning to knit so she would have a knitting buddy. That relationship blossomed into a regular stitch-and-bitch group, which sealed my fate as a knitter. I couldn't get enough of the books, the yarn, and the fun. Still, serious in those days was not like serious is to me now.

Ever since then, I've almost always had a knitting project on the needles, but for a long time only one project at a time and one project per year, because I knitted mainly on vacations or long trips. My productivity improved when I started reading the knit lists on the Internet. I learned about knitters who stole every odd moment possible to work on projects. There were people who knit at doctors' appointments, any meeting where it was allowed, in church, at long stop lights, waiting for chemo treatments. I was amazed. These people were truly committed. I started looking for my own odd windows of opportunity to knit. Soon, with the help of a headset phone I was knitting through any phone conversation longer than five minutes, stealing moments in the car and at my own meetings.

Still, with only one project going at a time, I sometimes wasn't at a point in the piece where I could knit on autopilot to take advantage of the time. It's not that I didn't have dozens of ideas ready to put to the needles, and there was certainly plenty of yarn around, but I suffered, as I think many knitters do, from a certain paralysis that comes from wanting to make the new project perfect. I would hunt endlessly for patterns and yarns that I thought went together in a unique and appropriate way for my knitting style and fashion sense, which was inevitably not the same as the designer had envisioned. Knitting only one item a year made this an important decision, and my exaggerated expectations often brought the process to a near standstill. Something had to give.

I was bursting with ideas I was too vain or timid to attempt because I knew my skills weren't up to the task. I had found more time to knit, but I wasn't knitting more.

When the U.S. invaded Afghanistan in the fall of 2001, the plight of the people in that country and in refugee camps made the news. My reaction was visceral. I constantly worried about these people, how miserable their lives were, how tragic the plight of their country. For some reason this, among all the world's tragedies and crises, struck a deep chord within me. I had to do something for the people of Afghanistan.

Winter was coming on. Sweaters, I thought: they need sweaters. Sweaters, mittens, socks, and whatever I and other like-minded people could send. Someone had to organize this. Someone had to see the same need and figure out how we, sitting in our comfortable living rooms in the United States, could help. The need to make a personal connection with the people there, to contribute something tangible, direct, and comforting, certainly couldn't be unique to me.

Luckily I found Afghans for Afghans, an organization run by the enthusiastic and resourceful Ann Rubin. The bonus was that she and the collection point for Afghans for Afghans were in San Francisco, close to home, and I could help with the sorting and packing of items as they came in. I had found my inspiration and the effect on my knitting was dramatic.

Knitting for others, especially those who don't care about color or fit or a perfect increase or heel turn, was liberating. The dozens of ideas that I had been incubating for years burst forth. Suddenly I was working on several projects at once and trying new constructions and techniques. I now had a project for every level of energy or fragment of time. I was released from my ego and the (imagined) criticism of finicky recipients among my friends and family. Compared to my previously constipated production level, I became a knitting machine.

It wasn't just quantity either. I was designing and adapting. I made a hat for the first time for Afghans for Afghans and wondered why I had never tried them before. (Living in northern California might have something to do with it.) Suddenly, I had new design ideas for hats too. I tried new stripe rotations where the pattern called for plain knitting. I added cables where there had been none and experimented with edging techniques picked up from recent reading. Feeling the urgency of another's need made my fingers fly through the knitting, lending them an intuition and skill I didn't know they had.

One great design challenge came from donations of vintage wool yarn. The colors were classic 1970s—harvest gold, avocado green, bright rust, and dirty brown—but I was oddly attracted to them and took a bag to play with. It was a real brain teaser to make something beautiful out of colors I found if not repulsive, then at least unsophisticated. The result was a stunning sweater, if I do say so myself, and many who saw it wanted one like it for themselves, challenging colors and all. I worked with the yarn endlessly on various projects, combining different colors, trying new trim details, twining it with other donated yarn, creating. The floodgates were open and there was no going back.

I looked for other unusual or orphaned yarns on sale to test my skills. How many odd yarns could I collect, combine, and make something beautiful? I kept a list of patterns with construction techniques I wanted to learn and worked them into Afghans for Afghans projects. I made my first Einstein Coat, falling in love with the pattern along the way.

I learned something else from knitting for charity. When you knit for others, you have the chance to knit a bit of yourself into the piece. Even I, an unrepentant multitasker, found myself alone at times quietly knitting, just knitting and thinking of the recipients, wondering about their lives, wishing them warmth and health and peace. Even though the Afghans would likely never know where the sweater they received came from I imagined my prayers went along with it and put a little good into the world. It was an opening of the heart.

I read somewhere about a study of potters. One pottery class was given the direction to work for a week and their final grade would be given on one object that they would submit at the end. Another class was told they would be graded on the body of work produced, not necessarily one piece. Not surprisingly the second class, churning out as much pottery as they could, produced the best work overall.

In the creative process, it is a given that practice makes perfect (or at least better quality) in the long run. Knitting so many pieces for Afghans for Afghans gave me the practice I needed to improve my skills and become a better and more fulfilled knitter.

I learned as I knit to be less harsh with myself, less demanding and judgmental. I started knitting a few pieces for friends and family too and, rather than meeting with criticism or polite acceptance, I found the recipients thrilled with the fruits of my labor.

I still work on those "perfect" sweaters for myself with sometimes less-than-perfect results, but they are much better than they used to be, a little closer to perfection, more expertly constructed, more creatively detailed and joyously worn. Knitting for those in need not only improved my knitting skills but gave me far more joy in my craft. Truly life-altering events.

Afghans for Afghans captured my imagination and touched my heart. May you find your own connections.

Yarn

Tzivia Gover

Carol brings string-thin needles and finger-
fat ones, circular for cuffs, and balls of coarse

yarn in a grocery bag. She has come to teach
me to cast on, loop the strand, wrap

like this. Pull through—not too tight; load on
the left, keep the ball on the right, purls

then knits; the simple knots that keep scarves,
sweaters, socks together. She promises

the ache my fingers make from all these stitches
will ease, and she tells me everything

as we shift rows. Magically more appear.
I remember macramé chokers I made in camp,

friendship bracelets knotted on bus rides,
lanyard key chains; how we girls passed secret

knots from hand to hand. Getting started
was always the hardest part. Girls

are always taking one long piece of string
tying it into one more thing. Pulling through

the loop like this. Not too tight. While we talk.
The baby-sitter who taught me to macramé

slippers. The hat I crocheted in the car,
as my lover drove. It's too easy

to say we braided something true and tight
into those projects. I envy the knots

boys practice: Knots for tying boats to shore,
hanging live things. Knots that slip free

at their command. I think: I could buy sweaters
cheaper. I think: I don't need another scarf.

I think: Where are those girls now? Where are
those friendship knots? Carol's gone

home to her husband. I survey an afternoon's
accumulation of slipped stitches. Crooked rows

Carol says will straighten in time. Still,
I command the days' loops to the needle's tip,

slip each row free and pull
a single strand, undoing all

those youthful stitches, too. Unravel
lanyard, wool, scarves, string, slippers.

I won't make a cable-knit sweater. Won't
macramé a dress with daisies down the front.

How Knitting Saved My Life

Ann Hood

In April 2002, I was basking in the happiness of my home, the unseasonable eighty-five-degree weather, the perils of training a new puppy, and the growing independence of my children: Sam, eight, and Grace, five. I had moved to Providence, Rhode Island, from New York City nine years earlier to start a family. My husband Lorne and I settled into a two-story red house built in 1792, on a street filled with other restored Colonials. The day we moved in, Grace dubbed it "the happy house." And so it was.

Then tragedy struck, as it always seems to do when we are looking the other way. Grace spiked a 105-degree fever and died thirty-six hours later from a virulent form of strep. Rare and inexplicable, this toxic shock-inducing strep has a high mortality rate among children, and it took Grace swiftly and horribly. Without warning, our family of four became a family of three. If ever a life needed saving after this loss, it was mine.

In the past, when grief struck or my heart was broken, I had always turned to words. Reading and, later, writing never failed to help me escape from and heal the wounds life inflicted. As a fiction writer and essayist, I had published many books that explored life's heartaches and challenges. But Grace's death was too enormous, too sudden, too hard to grasp. One day she was a vibrant little girl twirling in her ballet class; two days later a doctor was telling us that our daughter would not live.

Of course, I did turn to books for consolation. Friends delivered volumes of poetry and books on grief by the dozen. But when I read, letters no longer formed words, and words did not make sentences. Instead, each page held a jumble of letters that meant nothing, no matter how hard I stared.

A few months after Grace died, on a weekend trip to Portland, Oregon, for a wedding, I took a walk with my friends Heather and Hillary. When I told them of my frustration, of how words had abandoned me, they had the same advice: "Do something with your hands."

I laughed and told them how my hands used to sweat in home economics when we had to pin the pattern to the fabric; how I snuck home my paisley printed skirt for my cousin to add the zipper, how, during college, in a fit of love and passion, I spent months needlepointing a pillow for a boy. It came out so crooked and dirty from my sweating palms that I vowed never to waste my time again.

Learning to knit had never occurred to me before Grace died. Needles, thread, yarn, scissors—all belonged to a world that was not mine. When a button fell off a coat, it stayed off. When pants needed hemming, I paid a tailor to do it.

That fall Sam returned to the distraction of school. Lorne went back to the office where he worked as an estate planner, and although he often felt unable to work, his old routine and the needs of his clients kept him busy. And I faced the loneliness of every day without Grace.

On one such day, I opened the Yellow Pages and called knitting stores to sign up for a beginners' class. I had missed the start of most of them, and the others were held at night, when I wanted nothing more than to hold Sam and Lorne close to me. One afternoon, as I waited for Sam at his school, a friend of a friend ran up to my car, thrust a piece of paper into my hand, and said, "Call Jen. She'll teach you how to knit." Desperate, I called. Jen told me to come in on a Tuesday morning.

I learned to knit while sitting in a corner of a busy yarn shop in a seaside town, thirty miles from my Providence home. Jen, who ran her mother's store with humor and a cool efficiency, patiently talked me through the basics. Even after she explained, "Knitting is a series of slipknots" and I looked up at her in total bewilderment, she never grew impatient.

A week later, I was struggling through a scarf. I made a mess of it, randomly adding stitches, dropping stitches, then adding even more. When I showed up with this mess of wool, Jen pulled it off the needle and all my mistakes were miraculously gone. I could start anew. Unlike life, or at least this new life of mine—in which I was forced to keep moving forward through the mess it had become—knitting allowed me to start over again and again, until whatever I was making looked exactly as I wanted it to look.

Soon I became a voracious knitter. There were days when all I did was knit. Once, after nearly eight hours of knitting, I could not even open my cramped fingers. I knit socks and hats and scarves, and every part of me felt calm. The quiet click of the needles, the rhythm of the stitches, the warmth of the yarn and the blanket or scarf that spilled across my lap, made these hours tolerable. I made a red hat for Lorne, a blue one for Sam. I knit my cousins fluttery scarves for Christmas, and for myself, a scarf in Grace's favorite colors: pink and purple. I began a sweater. I learned to read a pattern. It quieted the images of Grace's last hours in the hospital. It settled my pounding, fearful heart. More important, knitting became a kind of prayer. I could spend hours knitting, and in those hours I could briefly escape from the grief that shaped my days.

Even now, nearly two years later, on Tuesday nights I still sometimes drive those thirty miles to Sakonnet Purls for a knitting class. Jen has moved to Chicago, and now someone else runs the class. Six or eight or ten women sit in a circle, on sofas and chairs, and knit. We don't talk much. I concentrate on manipulating four tiny needles to make a pair of socks for a friend who is sick. Our heads bent, from time to time someone moans, "Oh, no!" or shares her measuring tape or sighs with satisfaction. Here I am just another person who loves to knit, not the woman who lost her daughter. I am anonymous. Last Tuesday, a woman said, "I read somewhere that knitting is good for depression." I kept my head down even as I thought, *If you only knew.*

There is a story in Ann Feitelson's book *The Art of Fair Isle Knitting* about a storm that took the lives of eight Shetland Island fishermen in 1897. She writes that the women left behind, stricken with grief, supported themselves by knitting. "Focusing on the knitting in one's lap keeps death and uncontrollable forces at bay; it keeps one grounded."

Now I am kin to those women in Shetland, and to all of

those who find in the rhythm of the needles, the precision of our stitches, the weight of the wool, a way to keep death at bay, at least for a few rows.

In her poem "Wage Peace," Judyth Hill writes:

Learn to knit, and make a hat.

Think of chaos as dancing raspberries,
imagine grief
as the outbreath of beauty
or the gesture of fish.

Swim for the other side.

Slowly, words have begun to return to me. I still struggle to finish reading a book, or to write a page. But every day I pick up my knitting needles. I cast on, counting my stitches. Then I swim, Gracie. I try to swim to the other side of grief.

PART TWO

Who's in My Life

By Blood Knit Together: Women

Knitting Up the Raveled Sleeve of Care

Paula E. Drew

Coming into the kitchen, to my alarm I saw my little sister slicing a tomato with what looked like a very sharp knife. I ran over to her, grabbed the knife, and finished the job safely. Whereupon Brenda looked up at me and said patiently, "Paula, I'm fifty-two."

Of course I knew that. But I would always be four years older and somehow stronger and far less vulnerable; less fearful of injections, dentists, air travel, roadkill, sinister-looking strangers, bees, and caterpillars; less apt to be intimidated by officials; less devastated by humiliations; less traumatized by upheaval. I would also be less talented as an actress and musician and far less given to stage fright and agonized anticipation. But although I was the one better equipped to suffer slings and arrows, life somehow dealt her more pain and sorrow and more loved ones to bury.

Now, four years after rescuing her from one knife, I was taking the night flight from Newark to London to be at her bedside as she recovered from another—not a barely possible accident this time, but a grim reality. Not a kitchen knife this time: a surgeon's. After failing to answer phone calls or letters for several weeks, my sister had finally blurted out an apologetic understatement. She was not feeling very well.

I knitted furiously as the plane broke through a dark cloudbank into a rosy sailors-take-warning dawn over Heathrow Airport. My black Fun Fur yarn had rolled irretrievably under the seat in front, and I could only reel it in stitch by frantic stitch during the bumpy descent. The elongated trapezoid of the second sleeve was in its final stages, looking more like an Assyrian's beard than the scraggly mustache of its early stages. Early stages . . . Brenda's breast cancer was not in its early stages. It had spread to her lymph nodes.

Shuttle bus, Underground, mile-long walk lugging suitcase and knitting bag . . . I was ringing the doorbell of her Wimbledon house. Brenda came to the door, wearing jeans and a navy sweatshirt, holding a blue-and-white-striped mug of tea. She was supposed to be lying wan and listless on a daybed with hand-wringing husband and distraught teenaged son hovering in the background. But no, she was up and about, husband at work, son at school. It was, after all, ten o'clock on a Friday morning.

I longed to pour out my concern in action: propping pillows, adjusting footstools, chopping carrots, celery, and plump chicken into healing soup—but my sister, instead of lying back and smiling gratefully, was making me a pile of toast. As the weekend wore on, she did let me do the laundry and iron a few shirts, but to my dismay she seemed to be coping very well. Chemotherapy and radiation were to start on Wednesday. She was tired and a little apprehensive, but she was not trembling and hysterical and needing me to persuade her to come out from behind the gym lockers, as she had been the day of TB inoculations at school.

She felt very cold, but she couldn't wear the Lopi cardigan she'd lived in for years. It bothered her neck, which was swollen and tender. We had planned that cardigan over the phone. It was to have a patterned yoke in muted beiges and browns, with some dark blue here and there to make it more compatible with jeans. I'd already made a similar one for myself, cheered up in places with touches of red and green. I wanted to sneak in some vibrantly colored fleur-de-lis extensions to the outer border of the yoke, but Brenda was adamant. Though it stifled something in my soul to stick to the pattern, I made the cardigan exactly as specified. I added pewter reindeer buttons and mailed it across the Atlantic in a bubble-wrap-padded envelope.

Now, in her time of need, this old friend had turned on her and chafed her swollen neck. I could fix it. "Find me some knitting needles, about a 6 or 7," I said. But Brenda had no knitting needles. My circular Turbo needles with the flowing Assyrian beard were thicker than pencils. I poked through the kitchen drawers. No barbecue skewers—but there were some Malaysian chopsticks with red lettering carved into the shaft and counterproductive squared-off tips. I lowered each side of the front of the neck a scant couple of inches. Easing each stitch over the squared end of the chopstick with my fingers, I reworked the final rows of the yoke to avoid the tender protrusions on my little sister's neck.

Now I needed a crochet hook to make a new button loop

and to finish the front border on both sides. I had a cookie tin full of crochet hooks in all sizes at home, but not one in my knitting bag. In Wimbledon, you could get a tennis racquet at any time of the day or night, but not one of Brenda's neighbors had a crochet hook. With the point of a knife, I took the screws out of the earpiece of my glasses. Balancing the amputated frame on my nose, I made a loop of yarn on the hooked end of the earpiece. It made a rotten crochet hook, but it worked. Afterwards, Brenda said that she didn't think she would need the top button loop, as she would probably leave the top button undone. Could I perhaps take the top loop off again? I said "No."

Brenda's chemotherapy and radiation treatments are over. She has no hair, eyebrows, or eyelashes. I have just mailed her a black Fun Fur jacket exactly like mine, except that it has plain black buttons, not little pewter whales. The sleeve will be warm and soft against her swollen right arm. I hope she won't spill anything on it.

The Christmas Sweater

Lauran G. Strait

"Yuck, Mom. You aren't really going to wear that, are you?" Sixteen-year-old Annabelle, mouth open, tongue hanging out, feigns a retch.

"Stop being so theatrical," I say as I pull on a crimson cardigan adorned with a forest of nubby pines. "Be happy I'm not wearing the one with the battery-operated appliqué." I smooth a row of knitted trees across my stomach. "Maybe I should switch to the one with the running reindeers, prancing pine cones, and saluting Santas? What do you think?"

"The entire Christmas sweater genre is one gigantic fashion faux pas. It's hideous, Mom! I'm gonna spew." Nose and eyes squeezed into a sneer, Annabelle flounces on my bed.

"No spewing there. Go hurl on your own bed," I grin.

"It's not funny. I hate Christmas sweaters. They look tacky. More importantly, they make you look fat."

"Well, of course they do. So what?" Eyes averted from the sweater, I stand in front of the vanity, swabbing blushing powder across my cheeks. "By wearing a tacky garment like this, I'm telling the world that I love the holidays so much I don't mind looking like I've spent the year consuming nothing but sugar cookies and eggnog laced with rum."

Annabelle smirks. "What if one of my friends sees you wearing Christmas trees around your midsection? Trust me, Mom. It's not a pretty picture. You look like a candy-apple on a stick."

I wince, then sigh. "You just don't get Christmas couture. Imagine how surprised your friends will be come January when I've shed these sweaters and no longer resemble a Christmas dumpling. They'll wonder how I managed to lose all the weight over the holidays. I'll be the envy of them all. And so will you if you wear Christmas sweaters."

"Yeah, riiiiiight." Annabelle rolls her eyes.

"I am right, Little Miss Sarcastic. If we stand shoulder to sparkly shoulder now with people who don't give a figgie pudding about fashion, we'll be able to regale everyone with our dieting prowess in January. They'll call us genius."

She leaps from the bed. "You're insane. You do know that, don't you?"

"So?"

"And you know you're a fashion nightmare?" Annabelle frowns at her reflection in the full-length mirror.

"That's my job. As mother of a teenager, it's my duty to humiliate you in public whenever possible. If you're lucky, someday you'll have a daughter to embarrass."

"Cool."

"You know I'll knit lots of Christmas sweaters for my granddaughter."

"You have excellent taste when it comes to creating the most hideous ones." Annabelle tosses me an affectionate smile along with her purse. "Maybe we can find enough yarn to make matching sweaters. Wanna go shopping?"

"Only if you promise to remind me not to look in the mirror when I'm wearing one of these things."

Just Like Her

Brigitte Miner

Since before I can remember, I've looked up to my big sister. The proof is right there, in our family photo album: that's me, the baby, making googly eyes at Karen, the toddler. When memories began to bake permanently into my psyche, I recall clearly that she was my childhood idol and inspiration. When she drew, I sat next to her and said I'd be very careful not to break her brand-new crayons, because I was going to draw, too, just like her. When she started playing the flute, I had to, too. Calligraphy, swim team, hip huggers, French, rock 'n' roll, books, boys, bikinis . . . count me in, every step of the way! I even managed to skip sixth grade, just like her.

Of course, while I adoringly cut and pasted all of Karen's hobbies, pursuits, and achievements into my life, I was not picking up on the obvious: she hated being shadowed. No sooner had she taken a breath in a new direction than I was there, panting behind her. If she tried to set boundaries ("Don't you dare touch my flute!"), I found a way around them ("Mommy, can I have a flute, too?"). If I surpassed her, or got too exuberant, she immediately quit the pursuit in disgust or despair.

I was also completely blind to another fact that everyone but me saw clearly: my sister and I were radically different people. "Night and day," our friends and family said. In retrospect, I can see why. Karen was cute, cuddly, and curvy. I was bony and squirmy. Only one of my four grandparents could bear having me sit in their lap. People liked to pinch Karen's rosy cheeks. I didn't have pink cheeks to pinch, just freckled cheekbones. Karen loved the peace of her books. I copied her reading habits, but I wanted to live adventures more than read about them. Yet in spite of our differences, I never failed to feel insulted when I heard the "night and day" cliché. Obviously these people just couldn't see that my sister and I were just the same. I loved her! I adored her! I was just like her.

And so it went . . . until, at age twelve, she picked up knitting needles. My mom and grandmother taught her in minutes. I could see by her absorbed expression that this was another hobby we were really going to enjoy. I insisted on learning right away, that very second. But I was no good at it. The green-and-white acrylic yarn was supposed to turn into a lovely striped scarf around my neck. Instead, it made a tourniquet around my needles.

In the days that followed, while Karen produced row upon row of perfect little knits and purls, I tried desperately to rally, but trees needed climbing, ponies needed riding, and frosty winter and cold necks were so many seasons away. Karen beamed as I battled yarn and yearnings. She finished her picture-perfect scarf and started a more ambitious project: a yellow sweater with a popcorn texture—in my mind I called it "Buttered Popcorn." I gave up and staggered to freedom—to the trees and ponies—admitting defeat for that summer season.

Is it any wonder that my sister went on to brilliant knitting heights, leaving me in her dust? A faster, more perfect knitter there never was. For the past thirty-some years she has lost herself in lovely yarns, emerging with works of art for family, friends, and the needy. She knits every day. No pattern is too complicated, no needle too fine. Watching her, I wistfully imagine that she could, if she so desired, pull out a few of her white hairs and whip up some really fancy spider webs on size 0000 needles.

Mind you, I didn't give up knitting for good. Every so often I limped along on size 14s with some foolproof pattern. When I was in high school I decided to tackle my very first sweater (Karen had knit dozens by then). I chose acrylic mohair—this was before natural fibers were back in. I refused to do anything about the stitches I lost, even when they were pointed out to me. To this day, I do not undo rows, regardless of my errors. My mom, in pity, wove most of the lost stitches all the way up to whatever row I was presently at. This resulted in a unique texture of warped puckers. My sister dubbed my creation "The Animal" and smiled contentedly whenever I wore it. It was a visual reminder that I would never, ever catch up with her.

And so it went. Whether I liked it or not, I had come to realize that with the passage of time, Karen and I were going our separate ways. She ended up on the East Coast, married to a respectable scientist, with that perfect family scenario: two kids, two cars, nice house, a dog, and a closet full of yarn for 0000 needles. I spent some time in Europe, ended up on the West Coast, went through a nasty divorce, and made my house with my own two hands out of European adobe (aka mud). I don't have any closets of yarn in my house. For that matter, I don't have any closets in my house.

A few years back, my sister and I got together again. We put on a pot of tea. Before I knew it, she was getting the whole Little-Sister-Shadow thing off her chest. We laughed ourselves to tears—or maybe cried with some hysteric laughs mixed in. She pulled out her current knitting project, a beautiful sock that I could never hope to duplicate. I admired it, ever the adoring little sister. Then I scooted my spinning wheel over and started to spin the dog hair that she'd collected for me from her Sheltie, as she worked on her heel.

We're very different, my sister and I. I can't understand why people who see us together now say that we look so much the same, that our voices are identical, that we share so many common pursuits. I can't understand them at all. Can't they see how different we are? But no matter. What's important is that we love ourselves—and each other—just the way we are.

The Fabric of Time

Jenny Frost

My grandmother lived in a big, old, angular Victorian house in a small city in central Illinois on the shores of the Fox River. It is a place where time seems to flow along the river's banks with a smooth and easy current.

In my grandmother's front hall stood an ornately carved foot-pumped upright organ. It wheezed and groaned and thumped, but made a powerful, wailing noise that filled the house. At an age when "no" was a common word, I was allowed to play it, even though my feet could not fully reach the pedals. The front stairway to the second floor was lit by two large leaded-glass windows. Their prisms threw rainbow waves across the stairs. In the colorful lights, dust motes danced in the air. The house was suffused with a pleasant musty smell. My grandparents had raised their family, including my mother, in this house and had been in this place for a long time. It felt safe and warm and impervious to change.

Early each morning my grandmother padded in her slippers down the stairs to the kitchen. There she sat on an upholstered bench in the eating nook. The sky was still dark, but she was in position, quietly smoking a cigarette while playing solitaire or knitting. The kitchen was an island of light in the darkened, quiet house. It was our world and ours alone.

My grandmother taught me to knit. Sitting together, hour followed hour as I painstakingly knit row after row of garter stitch on my most recent scarf. We chatted about the worldly concerns shared by a small girl and her grandmother. My grandmother's fingers were long, the fingers of a pianist and organist, but gnarled and twisted with arthritis. They looked well used and very capable. With her sure touch, she guided me through the process and patiently picked up dropped stitches and set my work to rights again. Time ticked by very slowly in those hours. My grandmother's old black Seth Thomas clocks marked each moment's passing.

Now I sit with my daughter and guide her young hands through the process of knitting row after row. She nestles close to me as we discuss the worldly issues shared by a small girl and her mother. As I nuzzle my face against her long hair, I remember the hours spent knitting many years ago. I feel them as I hold her hands in mine. Knitting is the continuum as generation follows generation. Each stitch knits together the relationships that flow together, forming the smooth fabric of time.

My Mother's Hands

Kate Dudding

I love saying my mother's name out loud: Lucile Ellen Elliot Eike.

She called me her favorite daughter. Then again, I was her only daughter. But I'll return the compliment—she was my favorite mother.

She died in 1987. About ten years later, I started to worry that whenever I was remembering what she looked like, I was remembering only photographs of her. It seemed as if I had forgotten what she looked like through my own eyes. This really bothered me. I was afraid that she was slipping even further away from me.

But then I remembered her hands. And there are no photographs of them.

My mother's hands were thin; there wasn't much meat on them. You could see the bones and veins through the translucent skin on the back. She had long, slender fingers. She let her nails grow about a quarter of an inch beyond her fingertips and filed them into delicate ovals. She rarely wore nail polish but she always wore her platinum wedding band. As long as she wasn't doing anything messy, she also wore her matching engagement ring, with its round brilliant-cut diamond.

The more I thought about her hands, the more I remembered. Since my mother always had at least one knitting project in progress, I remembered a lot about my mother's hands and knitting.

My mother knit countless sweaters for my father, my brother, and me. She also made clothing for my cousins. When Lee Ann started skating lessons, my mother made her a long, long skating hat, with stripes of many different leftover yarns. This hat was so long that Lee Ann could wrap it around her neck a few times as a scarf if she were cold. When Laurel graduated from high school, she and my mother went to Cederbaum's, a yarn shop in Bridgeport, Connecticut, where my mother bought yarn for forty years. They picked out a sweater pattern and some orange mohair yarn. (Mohair was big in the early 1960s, you may recall.) When Laurel's brother Lance graduated from high school, he picked out some heathery, grayish blue yarn and an Aran pattern. Whenever my mother saw him, she'd whip out the sweater for a fitting. Lance wrote me recently about his sweater, "It's probably the only high school graduation present that I still have. It's up on my sweater shelf to this day. And whenever it's cold out and I need to wear something special, the handiwork of Aunt Cile still warms my body and soul."

My mother usually knit while she watched TV. She was fascinated by the U.S. space program. She watched all the Mercury, Gemini, and Apollo space missions on our black-and-white TV, knitting while listening to the voice of Mission Control. Once she was making me some gold mittens with a cable on the back. Knitting patterns usually give complete directions for the right side of the garment only. For the left side, the directions start you out, then say, "Complete this side following the directions for the right side but reversing all increases and decreases." During a particularly absorbing space mission, my mother forgot to reverse the instructions and didn't notice until she had completely finished making the second cabled right mitten. Luckily she had enough yarn to make me two matching left mittens. She rarely made mistakes like that, though.

My mother continued knitting steadily until two years after my father died, when she had an eight-hour cancer operation. When I saw her in the intensive care unit, she really wanted to tell me something, but with the breathing tube, she couldn't talk. It was difficult for her to write because of the drugs and because she didn't have her bifocals. She tried nonetheless. The only words I could read were "died," "father," and "sweater." Those words made no sense to me, although I did reassure her that she hadn't died.

Several days later, when the breathing tube had been

removed, she told me what she had been trying to say, but she wasn't so desperate to tell me anymore. It seems that sometime during her operation she thought she had died, and she had had a vision of life after death. Now it wasn't the standard one that you may have heard of, with a long dark tunnel with a warm, welcoming light at the end. In my mother's vision, she saw a river and my father standing on the other side of the river, waiting for her. But he was wearing a sweater that she hadn't made, and she wanted to know WHO had made him THAT sweater!

I asked her, not sure what the drugs might be doing to her mind, "Mother, you do remember that Father couldn't take any of your sweaters with him?"

"Yes, I know," she replied with a laugh.

So we discussed her vision and decided that there must be some sort of society of designated knitters in the afterlife that makes sweaters for people whose personal knitter has yet to arrive.

Yes, I remember my mother's hands.

I'm reminded of them when I look at my own hands; they're the same shape, even the moons on our fingernails are identical. My bones and veins are beginning to show through the skin. I'm reminded of my mother's hands when I see my sister-in-law Betsy's hands, because Betsy's engagement ring has my mother's diamond in it. I'm reminded of my mother's hands whenever I knit sweaters for members of our family.

So I'm not bothered anymore if I need to refer to a photograph or a tape to remember some physical characteristic of my mother. You see, I *know* that I remember my mother's hands. And I know that I remember my favorite mother too.

La Grande Traverse

Amy E. Tyler

I had to buy the wool, even though I was a novice spinner and it wasn't cheap. It was a perfectly prepared combed top, and the colors drew me in—blues and lavenders and bits of green. Liquid, a large body of water.

I let that fiber mature in my stash, waiting for the time when I would have sufficient spinning skills to do it justice.

That could have been a long wait. Instead, I spun it up last spring to knit a shawl for my sister Meg. We are only one year and five days apart in age. Practically twins. My older sister Jo used to call us "Meg the Egg, and Ame the Same." We had been quite close as kids, grew apart as teenagers, and then found comforting commonality as adults.

When I was twelve or thirteen years old, I became an atheist. About the same time, Meg embraced God in a most profound way. I was appalled by her willingness to follow orders blindly; she was probably appalled by my anarchistic tendencies.

Fortunately we both mellowed. She stopped trying to convert me to her brand of Christianity. I recognized that she had found a reasonably successful life path, although not one that I would choose. Independently we developed fiber addictions: mine for knitting and spinning, hers for quilting. I love texture; she is an adept colorist. We both can see ourselves spending a great deal of time together in our old age.

These days, I rely on Meg.

She was coming from Chapel Hill, North Carolina, to Omaha, Nebraska, to take care of me. I was scheduled for a bilateral mastectomy. Meg's a nurse. A good one. She was able to see me through the surgery and stay with me for a week. Meg told me that the attending nurse at the hospital where I'd had my surgery had said that I asked "Where's Meg?" the instant I came out of anesthesia. Meg was pleased.

For her help, and for her sweet spirit in general, she deserved a handspun handknit shawl. Besides, Meg's favorite color is blue. Mine isn't. The fiber was meant for her.

As I spun the wool, my thoughts wandered to the Grand Traverse Bay in northern Michigan, the corner of the world where my soul resides. I want to be there right now. I spent many weekends as a kid near there, and I was lucky enough to live in Traverse City for a couple of years. The water of the bay is invitingly blue and its fresh water is soft to the touch.

I found a stitch pattern that was wavy, both vertically and horizontally, and used it for a rectangular shawl. I gave the shawl a name, "La Grande Traverse." I believe that's what the French trappers called the bay when they first saw it. The Great Crossing. It was the right name.

A Knitting Legacy

Jennifer McCann

I have a picture here beside me, taken of me when I was only a small bundle wrapped in a receiving blanket. I have been set in the middle of a bed, and surrounding me on all sides are knitted layettes: jackets in yellow, green, purple, and baby blue, each with matching hats or hoods and two pairs of booties each. I am flanked by blankets in rainbow stripes, yellow, and green. Once I made it known that I was a girl, the dresses began to arrive. I arrived in September, and here is another picture of me, developed in October, in a pink knit dress with matching hat and booties. All this abundance came from a single pair of hands: my father's mother—my grandmother Betty.

Betty was born in 1924 in Brisbane, Queensland, Australia, the youngest of three sisters. Her mother and elder sisters were all avid, meticulous knitters. But Betty was told that she could never learn. My grandmother was born with a left arm that ended just past the elbow. Her mother refused to try to teach her to knit. But she must have watched her mother's and sisters' hands until she learned without the need for words. A small child in such a household would have picked up the rhythm of knitting, much as any child absorbs the language spoken around him or her. I can see her there, a small girl, studying their movement with the feeling of one left on the outside of something special.

When she was five, she walked all alone to the local butcher's shop, asked for meat skewers and twine sat down, and taught herself to knit.

I like to imagine her there, a small girl struggling with one hand, the other needle braced against her side. The gleam in her eyes, the concentration and focus it must have taken, the reward of seeing her first stitches take shape. I see her triumphant return home, twine in hand, to prove to her family that, yes, she could knit. She *would* knit.

My grandfather, an American soldier, was stationed in New Guinea during World War II. He met my grandmother in Australia. She was only eighteen when they married and she had the first of their two sons. My grandmother stayed in Brisbane with her family and waited for her husband to complete his tour of duty and return to live with her there. But he was soon wounded and sent to a hospital in America, and when the war ended he had no money to return. It was a year and a half before they were reunited; my grandmother took her two-year-old son—my father—with her, alone on the long sea journey to the United States. They never lived in Australia.

She was unhappy here, I have been told, although the only memories I have of her are of her smiles. She had a bottomless adoration of me as the first grandchild, and a girl, and I was simply and terribly spoiled. When I was two, she knit me six sweaters for Christmas. I am relieved to know that I demanded to wear all of them at once.

My grandmother rarely left her house, a fact I accepted as another aspect of her love for me. Of course she would always be there, waiting for me to come and visit her. I remember the sight of her there as we pulled up, sitting in her chair by the window with her brown knitting stand by her side.

I realize now that she must have been extremely lonely, so far from her family and country. She missed Christmas at the beach; she missed papayas (pawpaw) plucked ripe from her uncle's trees and eaten in the shade. She was painfully self-conscious of her missing arm. A small town can be terribly isolating; people stare, children are cruel.

Her knitting must have been a great comfort for her, a concrete act of creation, something solid she could hold on to and take with her. The feeling of the yarn in her hand was something warm and familiar, her fingers singing their song in a strange land.

My grandmother died when I was seven, her lungs full of cancer from the cigarettes she never let me see. I remember walking home from the school-bus stop on the day she died, scraping through the gravel at the side of the road at the end of a normal school day. I remember my surprise at finding my father there, how he sat with his arm around me and told me that my grandmother was gone. I rested my head in his lap, my child's heart numb. I knew I should be feeling great sorrow and hated myself for not feeling anything. I worked myself into tears, but real grief came only much later.

After Betty died, my mother kept her knitting bag and her leftover yarns. She left a stash of brown and evergreen skeins, enough for an afghan she had planned.

When I finally started to teach myself to knit a few years ago, I used her yarn and needles to make my first stitches. I thought of her and spoke to her as I struggled: *Grandma, I'm learning to knit. What do I do now? Help!*—whispered prayers to a private patron saint. When I finally managed to knit across an entire row, I was surprised to discover a soft familiarity, as if part of me was remembering how to knit, instead of learning for the first time. Maybe it was the "knitting gene" she'd passed down to me, or maybe it was a long-lost memory of watching her knit as I sat on my grandfather's lap. Either way: to me, knitting feels like a legacy.

Now I page through the notes written in the small spiral-bound pad tucked into her knitting bag. *Sue's red vest—good fit*. Or *pattern for booties & bonnet, cute*. But I like her unflinching record of failures: *Blue Cardigan, 1970—sleeves too long* and *Jenny's yellow vest—too small.* When I make my own mistakes, I look back at hers and remember that it can all be noted, learned from, improved upon. I don't hesitate to keep a journal of the projects I have completed. Someday, I think, maybe one of my descendants will look back through these pages finding inspiration for his or her own knitting and an understanding of what has been handed down.

I still wear the sweaters she knitted for my father when he was in high school, simple, classic designs: a V-neck in forest green, a brown cardigan. My son wears sweaters that she made for my younger brother when he was a boy. Some of her sweaters have worn down to a raveling; others remain in storage. They wait for another little girl to come along and have her picture taken, surrounded by knitted love, in a pink knit dress with matching hat and booties.

Clumsy

Marge Wooley

She had a quick smile, a big laugh, and a good word about everyone. Among other things, she was loyal, happy, loving, and kind. She was a devoted wife to my father for nearly sixty years and the best mother anyone could hope to have. But she was clumsy.

She fell down a lot. She fell in the downtown square of our elitist little New Jersey town; she fell on a trip visiting colleges during my sophomore year in high school; she fell upon entering the front door of a small country market. The list goes on and on. Often, her landing areas involved mud.

Her clumsiness wove its way through all that she did, including her knitting. Dropped stitches were a way of life. She called it "knittin' and rippin'." A good knitting session was when her work was a bit longer when she finished than when she started. She was my first knitting teacher and one of the first lessons she taught was not to get discouraged when "rippin'" was required. Together our clumsy fingers knit and ripped our way through scarves, mittens, hats, and (finally) my first sweater. These projects required many trips to Belle, the elderly lady who lived behind us, who was a lifelong knitter and the mender of major gaffes in our work.

Time passed, and I went off to college and abandoned my knitting for other interests. But my mother continued, with more simple projects like baby blankets. Her clumsiness led to interesting and erratic patterns in the stitches. Belle was gone by then, so those mistakes remained, but my mother didn't mind. The baby who received the blanket wouldn't notice or mind one bit, as it slept wrapped in the warmth produced by her loving if less-than-nimble fingers.

While I was away at college, she was working on a new project when she had another accident. She had put her knitting under her arm so that she could use her hands to brace herself as she sat down on the couch. As she did so, the blunt end of one of the needles struck the arm of the couch, causing the needle's point to pierce her right breast. Dismissing it as just another clumsy moment, she didn't think anything more about it until she noticed a lump near where the needle had entered. She waited for several weeks before becoming concerned enough about the lingering lump to see a doctor. After tests, it was determined that the lump itself was nothing to be concerned about, but right beside that lump was a tiny malignant tumor in the early stages of development. After successful surgery and follow-up treatment, we were blessed to have this wonderfully kind, caring, and funny woman with us for another seventeen happy years because (thank God!) she was clumsy.

Knitting for Mother

Marylou DiPietro

The first time around, it went with us across the ocean, healthy hanks of majestic teal flying above the Atlantic. It was the first time my mother and I had traveled abroad together. It was the first time I tried to knit my mother a sweater.

She had picked the pattern, the color, the yarn. Janet, my beloved knitting guru from our local yarn store, Putting on the Knitz, had measured and remeasured my mother's bust and the desired length from under the arm to the very spot where the sweater would start and finish.

I knitted on the plane in the middle of the night. It was a race to finish the back. My mother's sighs and groans accompanied my knitting, as if it was causing her some sort of gastrointestinal discomfort, severe acid reflux, an unbearable sense of loss and loneliness perhaps. Why might a person who is having a sweater knit for her act constantly annoyed? That was a question I was loath to answer. In fact, she had fallen in the backyard the night before and was feeling the consequences.

It seemed she would rather I give the two English blokes sitting next to us my undivided attention as they insisted on asking us foolish, trivial questions about the U.S.A. These rakish fellows, along with three hundred of their cronies, were returning to London from a pharmaceutical conference in Boston. Perhaps she thought they might offer free remedies for her aches and pains. I continued to knit, anxious to see something tangible grow from the long hours of sitting in my tiny allotted space. I knit like a fiend throughout the pill popping and gin-and-tonic-induced rabble-rousing, while my mother flirted shamelessly with the two hefty Englishmen, who were young enough to be her grandsons.

The back was three-quarters finished when we touched down at Heathrow.

Throughout our ten-day expedition across the English countryside, and then in London, I kept rustling through my cavernous, maroon velvet knitting bag and knitting four or five rows as if my life depended on it. Somehow the gentle music of the metal knitting needles dancing together kept me from losing myself altogether. "This is sanity," I thought . . . "This is the inner rhythm that keeps me grounded. These rows, these steady stitches will serve as footprints to my inner journey."

I was halfway up the front of the sweater as we started our journey back.

We missed the flight because Mom had roamed off to find a place to have a cigarette (but I was still at fault). We were both exhausted and cross. My knitting took on a desperate intensity. It was at once the gulf and the bridge between us, holding us tenuously together while keeping us safely apart.

Once home and struggling with an inordinate case of jet lag, I found my way back to my friends and comrades at Putting on the Knitz. Much to my dismay, we not only discovered that I had made several mistakes in the sweater pattern, but both front and back were much larger than planned. "This is huge," Janet announced. I'm an anomaly once more: the tense, stressed-out person who somehow knits loosely.

"There's nothing you can do but start over," Janet told me.

"But—but—I knit across the ocean and back. Doesn't that count for something? You mean all that time was wasted?" I accepted the news like someone who has just been told they need to euthanize their beloved pet.

"Unless you want to give the sweater to somebody else. You want it to fit her, don't you?"

Yes, yes, yes, of course I want it to fit. Who cares if I knit flying back and forth over the Atlantic? No one cares. Let's tear it out and be done with it. Let's not give it a second thought. I began to take the sweater apart, rolling it back into the neat teal balls it started from. It's only time itself we're unraveling. Time and the possibility of maternal love. Let's start over.

At which point my mother's refrain became "Are you ever going to finish that sweater? Why did you knit it so loosely? I can't believe you did all that work for nothing."

When the sweater is finally finished (for the second time), it is absolutely stunning (my words, not my mother's). A month or so went by after I had delivered the sweater when I received a call from my oldest sister, who is a professional seamstress. She told me, "Ma stopped by with the sweater you made her. I'm not supposed to tell you, but she wants me to alter the sweater, take in the seams, add shoulder pads, shrink it, do something. I wanted to talk with you before I did anything." My mother's shoulders, already slight to begin with, had drooped dramatically in her old age. The sweater pattern was for dropped shoulders, which made her feel and look droopier than she already was. I knew none of this until my sister called to report the dilemma.

"Give it back," was all I said. *I'll wear it myself if I have to*, I thought angrily.

Occasionally my mother asks where that sweater I made her "went to." I tell her I'm not really sure, which is the truth. I cannot for the life of me remember where I put it. I did, however, wear it a few times, even though the color and style were not exactly me. I wore it with pride and satisfaction, ready and willing to accept a barrage of compliments, if, by chance, they came my way. I remember that it smelled of stale cigarette smoke from the month or so that it hung in mother's closet.

Now I'm three-quarters of the way through my second attempt at knitting my mother a sweater. A perfect blend of soft cotton and silky rayon. I've decided to add random stripes to the otherwise simple pattern. Solid peachy-pink, variegated nectarine orange and pale pear yellow. I didn't bother to measure my mother this time; instead I confiscated a machine-made knit jersey that she claims fits her perfectly, using it as a template. The shoulders in the new sweater are definitely not dropped.

Nonetheless, I dread the moment of the sweater's unveiling. I dread the moment of rediscovery, the unbroken thread from one failure to the next. This time, the second time, I'm not so anxious to finish the sweater, for fear that I might sever that thread of disappointment and expectation and incompleteness that has kept my mother and me bound together from the very beginning.

The Red Blanket

Fran Corriveau

The grass under my knees is damp and new to green. The air is warm and the apple tree in our backyard is waiting for just one more warm day to bloom. I am an Indian scout again. My brother, somewhere behind me, waits for me to come back with information so he can lead the cavalry ahead through our yard. I slide through the backyard in my best Pocahontas regalia, an old paisley coverlet with a crow's feather tied to my head.

I see a flash of red from behind the apple tree. My mother is sitting on the lawn in the old canvas-backed chair, knitting. She has on an old plaid cotton housedress and wedge-heeled shoes with white anklets. Her dark hair is bobbed close to her head. I think she is beautiful sitting there. I steal closer for a better look and pop up at my mother's elbow.

"Geenun, what are you doing sneaking up on people like that, Lizzie? You half frightened me to death," my mother complains—but never pauses her knitting.

"What are you knitting, Mama?"

"Well, I think this will be a throw for the bed. Do you like the red?" She runs her hand smoothing over the growing mass in her lap.

"Red is nice. Could you teach me to knit sometime?"

"When you're older. I don't think you could sit still now. I think I'll bind it with blue. How would that be?"

Mama reaches out to pat my cheek. She ruffles my bangs, shorn on one side in a wild moment.

"I'll be glad when your hair grows out. Whatever made you cut it like that?"

I try to remember why I wanted to experiment with my hair last week but the memory eludes me: maybe scalping practice? But my burst of creativity has left me with a rather rakish look that my mother is not fond of.

To change the subject I say, "How did you learn to knit?"

She stops and lifts her chin. Her hazel eyes leave me and come back. There is a pause. A chickadee calls at the feeder.

"Well, I remember one day I was eating my lunch in the back room at the woolen mill with the other girls. We had all been working hard sewing and were glad to sit down. I had just finished my lunch when I noticed Mrs. Knight pick up a bag. She was pulling out her knitting. I watched her work at it for a while; she said she was making a pair of five-needle mittens."

Sensing a story, I settle on the grass, my legs propped against the tree trunk. "What happened then, Mama?"

"Well, I watched her knit for a while before I said, 'Can you show me how to make those mittens?' I thought if I could sew wool, I could learn to knit. Well, Mrs. Knight looked right at me and she said, 'Go get yourself some yarn and I'll show you how to knit. It's not hard.' So I went down to the five-and-ten cent store after work and I bought some yarn."

I roll over on my stomach in the grass to get more comfortable. "What color was the yarn, Mama?"

She pauses her knitting and her hand finds her chin. She is still for a moment, revisiting that earlier time.

"It's been a long time now but I think the yarn was gray wool. Yes, I'm sure it was gray. Anyway, the very next day, I put the yarn in a bag and brought it to work. After lunch Mrs. Knight helped me to cast on and she taught me how to do the ribbing around the wrist. I worked on it at home all evening and then I brought it with me the next day."

As though to remember better, she stops her knitting again. I wait more or less patiently on my back now staring at the sky, my legs waving in the air.

"That day Mrs. Knight showed me how to add on both sides for the thumb. By the next day I had finished the thumb and she was showing me how to start the hand. I went home that night and got almost back to the top. After that I was almost done and I stopped pestering Mrs. Knight every day. I finished those mittens pretty quick. I did a good job for the first time." Mama laughs. I watch the red yarn flash through her fingers; I believe her. She has always knit fast and well as far as I can remember.

"When you were a baby, a woman I knew sent me a pattern and I knit little baby sets up and sent them back to her. She would send me some money when she sold them. It wasn't much but I liked the knitting and it was a little extra money coming in. Dad was working on the screens at the paper mill so he didn't get much pay."

My mother smiles again. "People used to ask me how I knit those sets. They were really pretty. Then after your brother was born, I didn't take in any more knitting but I still always knit for myself. One time I made a sweater for you with a little hood on it and a heart-shaped brim. That sweater turned out so good. People were always asking how I made it. I told them I made it up. I didn't need a pattern for it. I just kept on knitting the hood when I was through making the collar."

The memory lengthens the flash of her bright smile. Then the smile fades and a shadow crosses her eyes.

"After the fire when we lost everything, I lost my yarn too. I was lucky to have the clothes on my back and my babies. We didn't have anything left, nothing, not a thing. People were good though. They gave us clothes and we found another place to live."

She is so quiet that I can hear the sound of the peepers down in the swamp. I pull myself to a stand and brush the grass from my legs where the blades have left a pattern. I hear my brother calling and I yearn to dash away to our game. I start to leave but then on impulse, I wheel around and run back to her chair. She lifts her face and I bend and kiss my Mama's cheek. As I run back to the game, I hear her knitting needles start again.

Expectantly: Our Young

Baby Blues

Adrienne Martini

Before my daughter's birth, I was, at best, a sporadic knitter, a dilettante in the world of fiber and needles. Every few moons I'd trek out to my local yarn shop, chitchat with the proprietress, fondle gorgeous skeins, envision luscious sweaters, and, invariably, buy just one hank of a luxurious yarn. Then, without fail, I'd knit a hat, which would take another few months to complete. The cycle would repeat.

It was always the same basic hat that would emerge laboriously from my circular needles, a pattern that required only the knit stitch and a robust appetite for monotony. While I would put my knit stitch (and my purl, for that matter) up against the best of them, I have never been known for my attention span. Half-finished hats would languish in my knitting bag, worked on only in odd little bursts.

When my pregnancy became obvious, the second question—the first always was "Boy or girl?"—was always if I was planning to knit some booties for the babe. My answer was always negative. "I only know how to knit hats," I'd say, and while that was true, my larger fear was that I'd never finish a project before the child was in college.

In June of 2002, after a fairly uneventful delivery, Maddy arrived. Then my life wobbled off its axis.

With first babies come many surprises. Most are delightful. Who knew, for example, that such tiny toes could be so perfectly formed? Some surprises are less pleasant. No matter how much newborn experience you have, the arrival of your own can't help but pitch your life into a disordered haze of little sleep, occasional panics, and constant demands.

Most new mothers wrestle with the baby blues, a brief postnatal period of mild depression characterized by roller-coastering emotions and disturbed sleep and eating habits. The blues resolve themselves in a couple of days. Except mine didn't. Two weeks after Maddy's birth, I had slept one hour out of the last seventy-two, could not get through an entire sentence without crying, and was starting to fantasize about doing something awful to myself, simply so that I could get a break from my misery. When I called my obstetrician for the tenth time that week, she urged me to go to the emergency room. Once Maddy was safely in her father's arms, I went. I wouldn't get out of the hospital for five days.

Rather than a case of the mild-by-comparison baby blues, I'd sunk into a big, fat postpartum depression fugue. After a brief stay on a regular hospital floor, I was transferred up to the psych ward, a place I'd never envisioned myself landing. Before this, my life was wonderful, full of a supportive spouse, a satisfying career, and spirited friends. But you can't escape history, the sages say, and my own hillbilly gothic roots are riddled with emotional instability. Rather than send a layette, my family gifted me with a tendency for clinical depression.

Odd as it sounds, my stay on the psych ward *was* a gift. It is not a place that I'd care to return, granted, but it was the place I needed to be. In addition to ready access to therapy, the ward also combated the enemy of the depressed person—free time in which to dwell on all of life's real (and imagined) problems. The ward would sop up these idle minutes, whether it was by assembling jigsaw puzzles, playing cards, or just talking to fellow patients.

Once sprung and home again, I was suddenly faced with filling my mothering downtime. Since I still couldn't sleep easily, naps weren't a viable option. Since Maddy preferred to nap on me, I would be pinned whenever she snoozed. My knitting bag was generally within arm's reach and my neglected hats provided the perfect panacea. Their simplicity was ideal and the monotony a moving meditation. I could pick one up and immediately know what to do without having to refer to charts or instructions. For those first few weeks, I churned out one every couple of days and took the baby for outings to the local yarn shop when my scant stash went dry. I began to feel like Dr. Seuss's Bartholomew Cubbins, knee-deep in five hundred hats. I gave a few as gifts and some to charity, and one still waits for the perfect owner.

Three months later, I discovered the perfect baby sweater pattern and itched to see my child wear something I crafted. The going was easy at first, consisting of stripes in garter stitch. Then my novice skills were stretched when it was time to shape the neckline and, later, when it was time to make the sleeves. Seaming and blocking were new adventures. The finished product was a wonder to me. Not only did it look pretty good, I'd finished it in plenty of time for Maddy to wear during her first winter. She, of course, looks adorable in it.

Lilacs

Grazyna J. Kozaczka

Her slim, gentle fingers moved slowly through the long strands of fine cotton. The silky yarn slid easily against her skin. She brought the small skeins up to her face and inhaled deeply the earthy smell of the fibers. And again she shivered, admiring the beauty of the palest, almost opalescent shade of lilac filling her entire field of vision.

This was the color of lilacs surrounding the house of her grandmother Julia. It was the color of the spring of her twelfth year, the last spring before Julia's death, the spring they spent together in the warm and sunny house when lilacs hid their greenery under the abundance and fragrance of blossoms, the spring when her grandmother still called her "a little crumb" or a "small treasure." The changeable weather of that spring with its thunderstorms and sudden shifts from summer heat to damp coolness contrasted with the sedate routine of their life together. Their afternoons were long and slow as they sat close to each other on a simple wooden bench in Julia's kitchen, the sweet aromas of baking mingling with an even sweeter fragrance of the lilacs wafting through the open windows. When Julia was not too tired, she would bring out her large wicker knitting basket, once for picking apples in the orchard behind the house, but now holding what seemed like hundreds of skeins and balls of yarn in various colors and several projects—scarves, socks, sweaters. Soon they were knitting companionably.

Her grandmother's hands seemed to dance to the fast rhythm of rapidly clicking needles while she laboriously repeated exercises—cast on, knit, purl, unravel and start over again. The silences between them were not awkward, but filled with the twittering of swallows under the eves and the buzzing of insects around the huge lilacs. If Julia was in a particularly good mood, she would hum softly and sometimes would even break into a song, an old one learned from her mother or grandmother.

Now she had to will her fingers to remember the long-forgotten motions. She had to prepare beautiful, soft, warm things for her own "small treasure," for her own "little crumb." She was not concerned. She had time, more than half a year to get ready. But she would also be reasonable. No frilly, lacy booties, sweaters, and hats; she would concentrate on making a simple functional blanket to wrap around the tiny body and protect it with love.

She began that evening working from one corner and increasing by a stitch along one of the edges with each new row. Garter stitch would look right. Her fingers moved awkwardly, but they remembered the movements. Yet when she fingered the first couple of inches of the new fabric, she was not pleased. Too stiff, too tight, too anxious. She could almost hear Julia's voice: "Always think of a person, think of your love for the one you are knitting for. This won't do. Rip and start over again." So she listened to her grandmother. She cast on again and began humming Julia's songs; her fingers relaxed and formed the stitches with increasing ease. The rhythmic clicking made her feel tranquil and content.

The pain came suddenly. It twisted her belly, shook her slight frame, and left her bewildered. Why now? The blanket was not ready. She had only passed the halfway point, at which she began decreasing by one stitch in each row. The newly formed corners looked neat, just right for tiny fingers to grab and hold. So why the pain? Not yet, not yet, my knitting is not done, she pleaded with every surge of pain and nausea.

Her doctor was reassuring. "It might still be fine. Put your feet up and come to my office in the morning."

She knitted through the night. She knew now this was not for her "little crumb," for her "small treasure." But it could still surround some other tiny body with the spring fragrance of lilacs, and the safety of Julia's love all worked together into a square of soft fabric.

Mondays

Cindy Monte

On a Monday afternoon in February, when I was fifteen weeks pregnant, I said to a friend, "I'm so afraid that I'll get to my midwife appointment tonight, and she'll tell me I'm carrying a dead baby." My friend said all the right things, that I was crazy, that there was no reason to think such a thing, and to stop worrying.

That evening, at the appointment, there was no heartbeat.

The next few days were a numb blur, as we went to the ultrasound, talked to midwives, doctors, anesthesiologists, receptionists, and scheduled the needed procedure for Friday morning.

Friday afternoon, my husband asked me what I wanted to do that weekend.

"I need to go to the yarn shop and get yarn to start a new sweater."

I picked a complicated Alice Starmore pattern, full of cables and bobbles, something I had little experience doing. I hoped it would take lots of concentration, help distract me, pass the time. I spent the weekend winding yarn, counting and twisting stitches, purling and knitting, getting through the hours and hours that make up each day.

On Monday afternoon, I was back at my teaching job, reading to the third, fourth, and fifth graders. I picked up the book I had been reading to them, *The Mennyms* by Sylvia Waugh (a wonderful story of a family of living, life-size rag dolls). We had left the Mennyms in the midst of a family crisis. I began reading the next chapter, entitled "Monday Afternoon."

"Granny Tulip was in the breakfast room trying to work out a rather complicated knitting pattern. She had made up her mind that if she worked hard at this problem, Appleby would be home before she had finished. It was pure self-comforting superstition, like not stepping on the cracks in the pavement. But it was a way of diverting the mind from an unbearable sorrow."

Eyes welling up, voice choking, I had to stop reading.

"What's wrong?" the kids asked.

"Oh, you guys, Granny Tulip knows what's what," I told them. Comforted and cheered by Granny Tulip, we read on.

Later that day, I shared the story and the beginning of my diversion sweater with a fellow teacher/knitter. She was concerned, "What will you do with this sweater? It will always remind you of this sadness. You'll never be able to wear it."

"I'm going to finish it. And I'm going to wear it next winter, pregnant," I said.

And I did. And I was. And on a Monday afternoon in May, Aidin Blue was born. Then, four years later, on a Monday in July, I gave birth to Owen Moon. Just as, years and years before, I had come into the world, on a Monday afternoon.

Counting Rows, Counting Weeks

Judith Ader

Today, as I watch my wonderful eleven-year-old son, sitting on the couch wrapped in a handknit blanket, it's hard to remember how tentative his life was before his birth. Fifty-fifty: those were his chances.

In early 1992, when I was thirty-eight, my first pregnancy ended in a miscarriage. My doctor assured me this was not unusual and probably had nothing to do with my age. One miscarriage did not indicate a pattern and did not need further investigation. Three months later I was pregnant again, with all concerns of any soon-to-be-new mother, and one extra: I was less than a month away from my thirty-ninth birthday. My age made this a high-risk pregnancy. I had an excellent obstetrician and was generally healthy, so I put my fears aside.

I got genetic counseling, ate well, remained active, and

took my vitamins. All genetic tests came back fine: we had a healthy boy. An ultrasound at sixteen weeks looked normal. I developed gestational diabetes but controlled it with a very strict diet. All things considered, we were doing fine.

The summer of 1992 was hot. Towards the end of August I started to experience contractions. They seemed strong to me, but how was I to know? My doctor thought I might be suffering from dehydration and sent me home to rest and drink plenty of fluids. At the end of my forced two-day sabbatical I felt fine. The contractions subsided, and I returned to work.

Things went well for the next couple of weeks, until early on a September morning, contractions woke me up. Unable to go back to sleep I thought a visit to the doctor's office would be prudent. Around 7:00 A.M. I called the doctor's exchange, planning to leave a message that I would be at the office when they opened at 9:00 that morning. Instead of taking my message the exchange patched me through to the doctor, who insisted that I get myself to the hospital.

My husband drove. I can't tell you what we talked about in the car, but I vividly remember what happened when we arrived. I was hooked up to monitors. My contractions were coming every five minutes. If I'd reached full term, I would be heading into delivery. But a child born at twenty-six weeks' gestation had little chance of surviving. I had spent the last six of those weeks feeling his kicking and movements. How could we stand to lose him? They diagnosed preterm labor and put me on a terbutaline IV drip. The contractions slowed to three or four an hour, but my heart rate increased. I felt like a racing car.

Once home, I was put on complete bed rest, with a terbutaline pill every four hours around the clock. You may think that lying in bed all day long would be wonderful. You could read, watch TV, and sleep. By day two I found myself with a sore back, worried and a little bored. I had ten weeks and six days before reaching the thirty-seven-week gestational goal. I slept well at night and didn't need to nap. Watching soaps was out of the question if I wanted to retain any brain cells for motherhood and my return to work. Reading was good, but not something I could do day in and day out. I had to find ways to fill my days.

I found a natural rhythm. I made my bed in the morning and lay back down on the bedspread to spend time with Dr. Penelope Leach on morning television. After this, I turned off the TV and hooked up to a contraction monitor for an hour, reading a magazine or a book to pass the time. I would send the monitor results to a nursing organization. If the results were good, I would take a quick shower, get dressed, and lie back down.

This routine got me to lunchtime. My husband had to work, but he left the fridge stocked with all I needed for lunches. I would eat while lying down on the living room couch and watching the midday news. At 4:00 P.M. I hooked up to the monitor again and read for another hour. My husband got home at 5:30 and cooked dinner. We ate, talked, and watched TV together as I lay on the couch, trying to keep some sort of normalcy in our lives.

There was nothing to do during the hours between lunch and 4:00 P.M., until I decided to knit a baby blanket. Knitting while lying down was not easy, but it would fill my afternoons. As I started to count my rows, I started to count the weeks.

Twenty-eight weeks found me only a few rows into this

blue blanket. If he were born now and survived, my boy would be able to open his eyes, turn his head, and move his limbs.

By week twenty-nine, I had knit twenty rows. It was a wide blanket and progress was slow. My son could react to sound now, but his chances of survival were still not good.

Thirty weeks: his digestive tract was almost fully developed. The blanket had sixty rows, give or take. I was moving right along.

Thirty-two weeks: the blanket had a hundred and twenty rows and measured twenty inches. His lungs were almost completely developed; he would be practicing breathing in the womb.

Thirty-four weeks: two hundred and fifty rows. His hearing was fully developed. I was having more contractions and had to take a double dose of terbutaline every two hours around the clock. I needed the increased dosage, but my heart rate had to stay under 120 beats a minute. It was a delicate balance.

Thirty-five weeks: his kidneys were fully developed. He would be close to eighteen inches long and almost five pounds, a viable birth weight. My doctor and I still wanted to have a couple more weeks for my baby to gain weight. A higher birth weight meant fewer possible problems. Rows completed were about three hundred and fifty. The blanket was done, but I went on knitting, adding another forty rows.

Thirty-six weeks: the blanket was a little over five feet. I was taken off bed rest. If the baby arrived now, he would be fine. I needed to regain my stamina before the hard work of delivering a baby and caring for an infant once he arrived. I still took the terbutaline every two hours during the day, but at night only if the contractions woke me. I was up and about and my life felt normal. The best part was that my child would live; he would be fine. The relief was overwhelming.

At thirty-seven weeks my doctor took me off the terbutaline. Two days later I gave birth to a healthy baby boy. He was nineteen inches long and weighted six pounds and fourteen ounces. We brought our beloved son home from the hospital in that blue knitted blanket. May it always wrap him in love and hope.

Pound of Love

Cathy Cooper

Annie Dillard once wrote, "How we spend our days is, of course, how we spend our lives." That can either be a frightening or a comforting thought. I choose to see the comfort in it, especially since I have discovered knitting and crocheting. Three things came together to transform me into a yarnworker: a Lion Brand catalog, a pregnant coworker, and a need to give.

The Lion Brand catalog offered the miraculous-seeming "Pound of Love," a generous skein in a cool minty green (an appropriate color for gender-not-yet-known). The pregnant coworker ensured that the free pattern included for a hooded baby blanket would be perfect. I was (literally and figuratively) hooked!

I work in a large advertising agency that guarantees a

nearly unending source of expectant colleagues. In just over a year and a half, I have made over sixteen baby blankets as well as twenty-one scarves, seven hats, two sweaters, and one sock. . . .

The making and the giving are inextricably linked. I savor the whole experience—choosing the yarn, the pattern, and the needles or hook, the sensation of yarn-fingers-needles and the finished project growing step by step, finally folding it into tissue paper (being sure to tuck in some dryer sheets for the sweet scent), picking just the right card and ideal bag or box; putting it all together; giving it away.

For someone who spends much of the day talking, reading, writing, and analyzing, yarnwork is a miraculous haven from the day-to-day. It is tactile (I dare you NOT to touch that alpaca/merino/cashmere yarn!), colorful (with dye-lot names like Groovy and Macaw), timeless, and time-bounded (just one more row tonight!).

My most memorable baby blanket, though, was the second one I made from "Pound of Love." I began it, flushed with confidence. After all, I'd made the pattern before. How hard could this one be?

I began the blanket just before the Jewish holiday of Rosh Hashanah, the celebration of the New Year. It is a time of sweetness and beginnings, a happy and precious time of the year each fall. Stitch after stitch, row after row . . . over and over and over. Crafting the baby blanket was the physical manifestation of a prayer for happy beginnings for the baby yet to be born, of connecting that baby to a community.

A week or so later, I had completed maybe two-thirds of the blanket as I rode the Long Island Rail Road an hour out to a party hosted by a colleague. It was perhaps only fifteen minutes after we arrived that our hostess took us on a tour of her home and backyard. As my husband turned the corner to go into the next room his shoe caught on the lip of the raised fireplace and he fell. (What still amazes me is how he maintained the grip on his cup of soda and held it upright so it did not spill even as he landed flat on his face.) Everyone clucked over him but he assured us that he was fine, fine, fine.

Twenty minutes later he asked me to walk outside with him. "I can't lift my arm," he whispered. My mind whirled in circles—what could be wrong, how bad could it be? I quickly made our excuses. I eked possibly another tight inch of the blanket on the train ride back and we hailed a cab to go to the hospital nearest to our home.

I hope none of you ever needs to go to an emergency room, but those who have know what I saw and felt. We checked in with reception at 4:30 and we didn't leave again until after midnight.

What kept me going was that Pound of Love. Stitch after stitch, row after row . . . over and over and over. Row after row, row after row.

And something surprising happened as I worked—one by one people would smile at me, or gesture, or tell me, "Oh, that's lovely." I could feel that each stitch was somehow providing a connection and a collective strength to all of us either suffering or waiting for word on those we loved. The teenage boys fresh from a street fight, the old woman looking shrunken and alone, the frightened couple who barely spoke English, the boisterous, the belligerent.

Because the yarn was sturdy and my fingers, in my anxiety, were racing on autopilot, the blanket grew quickly. And finally (nearly eight hours later) I was called to take my husband home—with his shoulder broken and his arm in a sling.

I sat up that night after both my husband and daughter went to sleep, beset by a compulsion to complete the blanket—to draw to a close the project as well as the day's experiences. And that is when I realized that the perfectly rectangular blanket I had been creating had somehow become more of a large mint green jellybean, wriggled and rounded and utterly uneven.

What could I do?

I folded it—carefully tucking dryer sheets in between the folds. Taped shut the tissue paper and tucked the package into a gift bag imprinted with pastel baby hands and feet. Instead of a store-bought card, I wrote a simple note:

"This little blanket has led me through good times and bad times, through joy and through pain. May this blanket keep you and your new baby warm and safe. With much love always. . . ."

Michael

Elliott Carpenito

I first met him in the disused physical therapy room of a rundown orphanage in Chişiňau. When they brought him in, I had trouble matching his face with the one I had in my photographs. He was wearing a knit yellow-and-green pantsuit and was frighteningly tiny and frail. He had a distended stomach and all his bones stuck out. His skin was nearly transparent and his hair had whole patches missing. Even though he was thirty months old, he was the size of a twelve-month-old. He walked to me tentatively. When the caretaker said in Moldovan "Go kiss your father," I knew he was mine.

I gave him a teddy bear, which he eyed suspiciously. Only when he realized that I had blueberry granola bars in my bag did he let me hug him. He sat on my lap and sank into my belly as his lips smacked when he chewed. I never felt so full, so important, so overwhelmed. While he sat there, I just kept smelling him and rubbing my head against his. It was primal. I had to share my essence with him and capture his. In what seemed like minutes, they were back and swooped him up, and I was ordered to leave. After a fast and harrowing trip to the courthouse, I was on a plane back to the United States without my baby. After holding him, the thought of leaving without him was unbearable. I just kept telling myself that he "was in summer camp" and that I would be back in two weeks to bring him home, for good.

Landing in Boston was exciting and exasperating. I was happy to be home and get things ready, now that I knew for certain that he was going to be here in a few days. But managing the time was going to be difficult. So I did what I always do in tough times (and in good times, stressful times, joyful times): I headed to the yarn store. This baby who had nothing must have the most perfect yarn. Soft, warm, colorful. I chose all shades of baby blues and cream. It would be cabled and patterned and complex, just as our journey was.

The first week was about nesting, getting ready, and knitting in the evenings as I showed off his picture and told the story of our visit. By the end of the first week I had completed half the back. Drafting the colors through my fingers, I was thinking about how they would feel on his skin. Would it be soft enough, would he like it, would it fit? He was a boy who owned nothing. Not a pair of underpants. Not a pair of shoes. Everything he had was communal. This sweater would be his first. I was clear that every stitch belonged to him.

By the start of the second week, the pretense that he was "at summer camp" wore off. My anxiety was high and I began telling people that he was held captive by a hostile government and I needed to rescue him Rambo-style. I had visions of stealthily breaking in and grabbing him from his cradle, using my knitting needles as weapons of mass destruction if anyone dared to stop me. I could hear the animated bluebirds singing about us as we crept out in the middle of the night. Then I would come back to reality and continue maniacally knitting. I finished the rest of the sweater in two days.

I still had four days to go. My bags were packed and there was nothing to do but wait—and knit. In those four days, I finished his denim blue zip-up cardigan, and his orange, red, and green chenille crew neck. No sleep, just knitting. Finally, I got on a plane.

After an emotionally draining, physically exhausting week with a toddler in trauma being cared for by a parent in crisis, we flew home. He was a champ. He made it almost all the way home. Ten minutes before landing in the United States, he got violently ill several times. Unfortunately, everyone around us was in the firing line. I had to strip him down as I kept apologizing to everyone around me. The flight attendants were so kind when I stood up, holding him high in the air, yelling "Puking baby!" as I headed for the bathroom door, and "Save the *Visa*!" to the other parents traveling with me. They cleared the aisles and gave us a tablecloth from first class to cover him.

On September 30, 2003, at 2:07 P.M., my son Michael Anthony became the newest American citizen, wearing only a diaper, a tablecloth, and a soft warm blue sweater.

Of Love and Loss and the Sweater Curse: Mates and Lovers

Stitches

Katie Chilton

During the war
which ended
before we were born,
women in Japan embroidered
sennin-bari,
belts-of-a-thousand-stitches:
wide lengths of white silk,
each with one thousand red stitches
sewn by one thousand women.

Knotted into each stitch
a wish, a prayer—some given
by family, neighbors, friends,

others begged from passersby
or bought from vendors on the street
until at last there were
one thousand stitches
and then the men wore
the belts wrapped close
around their bodies, flying
circled in a thousand prayers.

I will knit a garment
of a thousand stitches,
ten thousand stitches, thirty thousand.
Each stitch my own incantation
binding us together
and keeping you from harm.

Happy Mother's Day!

Alison Jeppson Hyde

Last night my husband and I went out to dinner with some friends. Their kids are small; ours are in high school and college, and so one of ours was babysitting theirs.

After we ate and visited, we decided we all needed to hit the grocery store on the way back, so we might as well do it together. My husband pulled out his cell phone and called our daughter: "Michelle. What are you planning on cooking for your mother tomorrow? What do we need to pick up? I'll help you with the . . . Okay, okay . . ." They went on in some length and detail, some of which they managed to carefully make it so I wouldn't hear. Interspersed with an aside to me: "What do *you* want, dear?"

"Not to have to clean up after you guys."

He got off the phone. The other dad, who can't boil water in the microwave, was growling as he drove, "Remind me never to double date with you on Mother's Day eve again!" His wife was grinning with all the plans she now had for him to do for her. Ah my, the ways we get our comeuppances. . . .

This morning I realized I'd forgotten to tell my doting family to can the breakfast-in-bed cliché. Please! Okay, I sit there with this huge, heavy wooden platter uncomfortably and precariously balanced across my knees, in my room by myself, while everybody else is enjoying each other's company in the kitchen. Oh well, then, I guess I'll have to humor them, I decided. I knew from experience that I'd better lock the door first and shower and dress before they came in; last year they'd decided to do blueberry and sour cream blintzes and it had taken them hours.

So I did. I even remembered to unlock the door when I was ready. Then I sat there in bed with my latest knitting project in my hands, dressed in a warm wool skirt (the coldest winter Mark Twain ever spent was a summer in San Francisco, right? Brrrr today). I knitted. And knitted. And knitted some more. I was quite pleased that I got about twenty rows done on a lace scarf, which, thank goodness, was in a simple pattern so I wouldn't have to sneak across the house to grab my instructions from my usual knitting perch—that path would have taken me right past the kitchen. There would have been no end of teasing and reminding about other Mother's Days.

There would have been comparisons with the late-night Christmas Eve when the kids were little and my husband had set up a motion detector connected to a tape recorder; it was set to click on with his voice, saying sternly to whichever kid was sneaking out past the end of the hall to look at his goodies, "GO BACK TO BED, RICHARD!" (We knew full well which kid it would have been.)

As my hands worked the soft merino, I thought, *What a treat to knit before nine o'clock church*. I almost never get that. We let ourselves be in too much of a hurry. Holding the slender needles, the meditative repetitiveness of the pattern and the stitches had a soothing quality that helped put me in the frame of mind for the coming meeting. I'd have to do this more often.

My family finally came in. With one lonely and very small pancake, after all this time. Ten minutes before we had to leave! My son had burned the rest because they'd all been distracted reading the Sunday comics pages. Noooo, you guys, that's such a cliché, tell me you didn't do that! But they did. Just one survivor, served proudly on that platter with a miniature pitcher filled to the tippy tippy top with real maple syrup to drown the poor thing in. (After all, for a teenager, the sugar is still the most important part of the meal, anyway.)

I knew full well what was coming the moment I saw it. I had just enough time, as they set the platter down, to exclaim, "No!" and throw my knitting across to my husband's side of the bed, towards safety, before that platter landed and the pitcher toppled across me. It's a good thing for their sakes I saved my project! Good old wool: the syrup beaded up on my skirt, and I thought, if I run to the shower fast enough and shake it like a dog, it'll be okay.

But there were people in my way. One my six-foot-eight-inch husband, one my six-foot-nine-inch son—that's a lot of mass (particularly the husband).

"MOVE!"

They thought I was being unfriendly and decidedly crabby when they'd gone to all this hard work. They'd made a double batch, and even if none of the rest of it was edible I could still at least be a little grateful.

"MOVE!!!!!"

Too late. The syrup had soaked in. The skirt was toast. Or was that pancaked?

I wonder how that other couple is holding up.

The Shawl

Marilyn Webster

I sit here knitting an ivory silk tank top for a friend. My sister's house, where I am pet-sitting until I can move into my new home, is quiet except for the gentle summer wind and the occasional sounds that set the three dogs barking—drivers who decide to turn their cars around in front of this house, dogs out with their companions, skateboarding teenagers, and an elderly woman in her motorized wheelchair. Although I am counting stitches, my mind wanders, and questions about my future, the wisdom of this move, a phone conversation with my distant partner, surface.

I am aware that I am *not* knitting the shawl I started for my partner five months ago. This is in part because the day is too hot for a merino and mohair blend. But it is more than that. I started it the day she left. As she headed east along Interstate 40, I headed for the yarn store. Inspired by the shawl-knitting ministry, I searched for the perfect yarn to knit her a shawl. Something soft and inviting that I could knit on large needles. Something with character, but not too fancy or frilly. Something blue. I settled on two yarns, a variegated mohair with blues, greens, and a little purple, and a merino in shades of blue.

I planned to fill the shawl with prayers for her, for us, that we would find our way back together even though we would be living on opposite sides of the country—she in the Northeast and I in the Southwest. We'd made the journey together only seven months earlier on account of an important job opportunity for me. Neither of us had ever wanted to live in southern California, let alone Los Angeles County, but we packed our belongings, gave away furniture, rented out our beautiful home in western Massachusetts, and drove three thousand miles to the dry, hot Santa Monica Mountains. It was an adjustment in every way—the climate, the landscape, the people, the values, the prices, the traffic—and my partner was absolutely miserable. She hated everything, particularly her job, and was unhappy in our relationship. It seemed best that she return home.

Once back from the yarn store I curled up at one end of the sofa, did the necessary calculations and began knitting. The large needles felt awkward and were a little sticky, but I eventually found a rhythm that allowed me to pray. I have long appreciated the calming, meditative effects of knitting, but using it as an intentional contemplative practice was new.

I prayed for my partner's safe journey. I prayed for her happiness. I prayed she would finally sleep well after suffering from insomnia for a year. I prayed that she would jog and play her guitar and not work too much overtime. I prayed that living alone would teach her what she wanted to learn. I prayed that this separation would not mean the end of our relationship.

This shawl is not the first gift I've ever knit her. Although she hates coming with me to wool stores, she loves what I've knit for her—numerous pairs of socks, two vests, a chenille scarf, and fingerless mittens. She has waited patiently while I count stitches or finish a row. She knows that I swear at least once during every project.

One evening I put the shawl down. Why was I putting so much energy into this when I was in such pain myself? In truth, I wanted someone to make me a gift filled with love to comfort me. And then I realized that such a gift would not take away the pain. I folded the unfinished shawl into the brown shopping bag, placed it in the corner, and wondered what gift I could make for myself.

Over the next few months I learned to cook for one again, to ask friends to walk my dogs when I had to work late, and to strike out on my own adventures. I stopped crying every time my mind wandered to our relationship. I did not renew my job contract and decided to move to northern California, closer to family.

My partner came back for my fortieth birthday and lovingly cleaned my car, washing off the desert dust and vacuuming months of accumulated dog hairs, beach sand, and chewed fingernails. She wanted me to have a clean vehicle for my journey north where I would be looking for a new home. Good energy for a new beginning, she said.

Over the years I have grown good at completing projects although not always before starting the next one. But this shawl haunts me. The pattern is simple, but the process is difficult. As long as the stitches remain on the needles, my relationship remains open. I am afraid that by finishing it and binding off the stitches, I will also end our relationship. At the same time I long for some kind of resolution.

A fly buzzes around the room and the dogs try to catch it, bringing me back to my sister's living room. It is time to pick up the shawl again. After all, I purposely brought it with me so I could work on it during this transition time. Even if I'm still not ready to finish it, the process is part of my healing. The real gift is learning to trust and let go of the outcome as I give thanks for the time and love we have shared; let the memories, tears, and smiles come.

The Scarlet K

Jenny Feldon

I've been unfaithful.

There, I've said it. The truth is out; already I feel better. The rock of guilt lurking in my stomach feels a little smaller. It's time to absolve myself and confess this sin.

I'm knitting for another man.

The affair started in spring, during those first exhilarating weeks when the air smells like rain and clean laundry, and the sky sloughs off its gray winter pallor to reveal an exuberant blue. A time, certainly, when anyone's judgment could be impaired by the heady optimism that accompanies a change of season in New England.

I was having dinner with Scott—my writing professor–turned-mentor, a journalist almost twenty years my senior but a soul mate when it comes to conversation, literary and otherwise—at a Japanese restaurant halfway between his house in the suburbs and the city apartment I shared with my fiancé. We were drinking a bottle of chardonnay he'd brought along and eating sashimi and pickled ginger when the conversation turned to knitting.

"Will you knit me something?" Scott asked, stirring a chopstick in his dish of soy sauce.

"Sure," I said. I love to knit for other people, mostly because I become bored with projects as soon as they are close to completion. A true "process" knitter, I crave new horizons, better colors, larger needles or smaller needles or stripes or cables or yarn-overs. Knitting for friends and family means I don't have to look at a finished object once it's done; the newer, shinier project takes residence in my knitting basket and I forge ahead, no yarn attached. Until this pivotal moment, however, no fiber challenge had ever challenged my moral fiber. How could I have known that scandal lay ahead?

What he wanted, Scott explained, was a red hat with a white stripe in the middle and a folded band at the brim. A hat to match a pair of mittens he'd been given as a child, a gift from a woman on his paper route that he didn't appreciate until he was much older. The project appealed to my sentimental side and I readily agreed, prattling on about yarn weight and round versus flat while Scott looked blank and tried to share my enthusiasm.

When I got home, Jay was in bed, glaring from behind a magazine.

"How was dinner with your boyfriend?" Jay has never understood my friendship with Scott. An adamant reader of magazines and nonfiction (he calls fiction "fake books"), Jay can't comprehend my need to discuss literature and writing with a seasoned critic who's familiar with my work and my weaknesses. But he grudgingly accepts my dinners with Scott. Although our meetings are entirely innocent, an illicit pall lingers over them for reasons I can't quite explain.

So several days later, as I browsed the shelves at a local yarn store, comparing merino and alpaca, fingering samples and doing yardage calculations in my head, I balked when the owner asked me what I was making.

"A hat," I said. Blushing.

"A man's hat?" she replied, smiling and glancing knowingly at the engagement ring on my left hand. "You do know you're not supposed to knit for a man before you're married, don't you?"

I nodded yes, ducked my head further back into the hood of my sweatshirt, and hastily paid for my selections. Shamed, I left the store and shoved the plastic bag deep into my purse, hiding the evidence.

In truth, I had knit for Jay already, long before we were engaged. His blue-and-gray-striped, fringed scarf was the first project I ever completed. I knit the scarf in secret, late at night by the greenish light of the television after he'd fallen asleep, and on my lunch break at work, spooning soup into my mouth after every three or four completed rows. The look of surprise and pleasure on his face when he opened the gift is a priceless memory. He wore it beneath his overcoat on wintry days and I beamed with pride, knowing the work of my own hands protected his throat from the wind and cold.

At home, I pulled out my purchases. I can never wait to

start a project; I crave instant gratification in all things, and knitting is no exception. I wound the skeins around my wooden swift, crafting symmetrical balls. I scanned the pattern, selected a size and cast on. And then I felt the rock forming in my stomach.

The red yarn stared back at me from the needles. The color, rich and vibrant in the store, now looked brazen and tawdry in the lamplight of my apartment. I reached a hand to my stomach, feeling for the lump. Ridiculous. There is no such thing as knitting adultery. I began to knit, defiantly, my normally even stitches becoming tight and erratic with emotional unrest. I ripped out and started again. Cast on, count stitches, join the circle, ignore the lump. There is no such thing as knitting adultery. A tortured hour passed; my resolve weakened. I gave up and shoved the project in the back of my sock drawer. No need to have it in plain view, mocking me from the basket under the coffee table.

Weeks passed, then months. Summer came; no need for socks . . . and so the hat lay silent and unnoticed in a forgotten drawer. Waiting. Until today, when an early September chill made me crave the comforting heft of jeans, sweater, boots. I reached into my drawer for a pair of raglan socks—hand-knit, of course—and felt it.

Oh.

There it was, the palpable proof of my transgression.

I fingered the soft wool. I could practically hear its siren song. I succumbed.

And now here I sit, waiting for Jay to come home from work, knitting for another man. An adulteress of craft, guilty of betrayal on a level not sexual but surely physical. I will confess, I promise myself as I work the scarlet strands between tainted fingers. I'll tell Jay the truth. And maybe he'll understand.

The turn of his key in the lock makes me jump. My heart pounds in anticipation. I fight the urge to bury the hat underneath a cushion. Cross-legged on the couch, knitting in full view on my lap, I await his judgment.

"Hi honey . . . ," Jay says. His voice trails off; he spots the knitting. "Who's that for?" He knows, of course, that it isn't for him; he hates both hats and red. And as I open my mouth to purge my guilty soul, I see it.

Sticking out of his coat is an unfamiliar scarf. Green and yellow and white. No fringe. And peeking from beneath his lapel, an unmistakable square blue label. GAP.

I close my mouth. Jay follows my gaze down his own chest.

He hangs his coat—and his scarf—on the hook by the door. And I pick up my knitting.

Under the Lamp

Corey Mesler

Under the lamp
my wife sits knitting.
Her hands form a small cap
to be given to our
daughter's friend.
Her face is lovely in repose.
Her concentration

is starlight.
The cap unfolds like a tiny
life, one I almost missed.

Back Porch Knitting

Julia LaSalle

Some strange cicada makes a clicking noise. From our back porch, I answer with my own call—the sound of my knitting needles. Knit one. Purl two. The bug and I drone on.

The cordless phone is here, but it won't ring. Larry's working late, again. He has stopped calling to announce that fact.

Across my tomato plants and past the fence, our neighbor is doing something in his yard. He's about my age, and good-looking enough. They only moved in a few months ago, but I've noticed his looks before. I can see him through the pickets with a bandanna on his head and a shovel in his hands. I'm pretty sure he doesn't see me though.

His kids must be getting ready to go to school soon; buying notebooks and lunchboxes. Fall is just around the corner.

My tomato plants are almost done now for the season. Though a few tight green balls still hang on, I can tell from the dropping leaves, that they won't make it to red.

I study my knitting, the blue-gray yarn, and spot a mistake. I tear out my mistake and then keep going. Undoing more than is necessary. I can't explain why.

"Hey, neighbor," he calls. Startling me.

I look and see him leaning on the fence. His shoulders span

four of the pickets. He is very broad. I think he works in construction.

"Hi," I call back. "What are you working on over there?"

"Dead shrub," he says, "Putting a holly in instead. Mind if I come over?"

"No, of course not." Though he's never come over before.

He walks down the fence line and reappears next to my tomatoes. He walks around them and sits in the other porch chair.

"So, what are you working on?" he wants to know.

"Nothing fancy," I say. "Just a hat."

"Oh. That's nice."

I smile. Wonder what he's up to?

"So, are the kids ready for school?"

"Yeah, I guess." He leans forward, puts his elbows on his knees, and turns his head my way, brown eyes taking in my profile. "Honestly though, Crissy takes care of most of that stuff." He swivels his head the other direction. "We like to do separate things."

"I see."

"Actually," he says, swiveling back, "we're doing a lot of separate things lately. In fact, we're separating."

"Oh."

"It's not working out."

I take a deep breath; ask why. He doesn't answer. I keep knitting. Wait for him to start again.

It takes a while, but then he says, "I haven't actually told this to anyone else yet. I mean we know it, but I dunno. I think it started when we had our bathroom redone. It's a small enough house already. Then not to have a shower . . . Add to that all her screaming and bitching. It's ridicu—"

He stops himself.

"Everyone gets angry in a small house," I say clicking my needles with the cicadas. "It's understandable."

"I know," he says, "It's completely understandable." He turns his chair to face me. "The thing is, I'm just sick of understanding. I want a more quiet kind of girl."

"I see."

I know one thing is true: many nights I've heard her angry voice pouring through the screen door, but I've yet to hear his. Honestly, I noticed that back in July.

I'm careful to keep my eyes on my work, but know that he's looking at me. I finish a row. I turn the piece over and see his hand at the bottom. Underneath my number 7 needles, I see his hand in my work; and it looks enormous.

He twists the tail of my yarn in his fingers.

"This is beautiful," he says.

I've never seen a man's hand in my yarn before, let alone a hand like this. I can't stop looking at it.

He moves his fingers down my yarn and onto my knee. His big hand covers it, and that makes me feel small, not thick and turning a childless 34, but petite and thin, like a hopeful 26. It's nice. His hand saunters up my leg. I watch it saunter. He leans in closer, and says, "You seem so peaceful."

I put my needles together and wrap them inside my work, hold the bundle in one hand.

He moves and kneels before me. With his left palm, he covers my hand and my work.

I think about my Larry and the holly that these enormous hands are supposed to be planting. I wonder what's happening here.

"My mom used to do this," he says, squeezing both my hand and my work. "Made Kayla yellow booties before she died." Before I can help myself, I squeeze his hand back.

I pull my gaze from his hands and look at the face at my knees. His eyes look so soft. I can smell my wilting tomatoes in the air.

Suddenly, I know what he's doing here. I put my empty hand on his face.

"Honey," I say, in the strongest, gentlest voice I know, "I'm not your mom. And you, even if I did want to—you don't want to leave your wife."

"Oh, no," he says, "You misunderstand." He starts again to caress my thigh. I can see the stubble around his lips, and wonder how long it's been since I had the feeling of a first kiss. I'd like to have just that kiss, just that much. But know better.

I let go of his face, and pick up his hand off my thigh.

"Wait," he says looking up at me, but I don't wait. I feel sure.

I tell him, "Now I'm gonna say what you came to hear. Honey, it's time to go home. Be patient and plant your holly."

He stands up. Dismissed. He walks past my tomatoes and around the fence.

I open my work and start the next row.

Knit one. Purl two. Try not to wonder when Larry will come home.

Plan B

Michelle Mach

"It's like yoga," my mother said.

That should have been a clue. A few years earlier, I had

collapsed in sweating exhaustion after my mother had convinced me to try a "few" yoga positions.

Now she expertly cast on a row of stitches in chunky plum-midnight yarn and handed me the needles.

I sat hunched over a single row of ten stitches. My neck hurt and my fingers felt stiff.

"This. Is. Not. Relaxing," I grunted through clenched teeth. My mom had wheedled me with soothing promises of relaxation and my own beautiful knitted wardrobe. She reminded me that ten-year-old kids could knit. I had a good twenty years on them, I reasoned. How hard could it be?

"I'm done. That's it." I had finished two rows.

"I'll bet Neal can knit."

Neal is my boyfriend. My mother probably thought that statement would spur me to greater knitting achievements. I can be pretty competitive and I love proving people wrong. Instead, it gave me an idea.

That night I tentatively asked Neal whether he'd like to learn to knit. He jumped at the idea. "I've always wanted to learn how to knit!"

"You have?"

Why was I surprised? This was the man who not only knew how to wield some decidedly masculine power tools but also the sewing machine. Once he even sewed a fabric octopus—without a pattern of any sort—to stretch across his office cubicle in lieu of a Do Not Disturb sign.

Neal was a terrific knitter, just as I suspected. After a few minutes, he was quickly knitting row after row of even stitches. He finished his practice potholder and quickly knit a flawless second. "I think I'll make a scarf."

The scarf grew longer and longer as he continued to knit

throughout the fall. I leaned over and felt the softness of the scarf against my cheek. "It's beautiful!" I gushed.

"It's relaxing," he said, as another perfect row of stitches appeared.

This plan was working even better than I'd dreamed. He was relaxed. I was relaxed. And soon, I would be the proud owner of a beautiful hand-knit wardrobe.

Before long I was dragging Neal to craft stores for more yarn. I showed him pretty patterns of hats and sweaters. I found a canvas bag the perfect size for holding his knitting supplies. He finished one scarf and started on a second. Gradually, the project at hand became less interesting than the future projects floating in my mind. Now when he sat down to knit, I hovered over him. "Maybe you could make a sweater for me? Or mittens? How many rows does that make? How many do you have left? Are you almost done with that? We could set some goals. How does at least ten rows during every day sound? For your next project, I thought we could—"

Then one day Neal sat on the sofa and turned on the TV. The knitting stayed in the drawer. He was halfway through another beautiful scarf.

"Aren't you going to knit?" I put my hand on his forehead. "Do you feel OK? Can I get you anything?"

"I quit." His eyes stayed focused on the TV.

"What?"

"I don't feel like knitting."

I pondered this new development. There was no soothing click of the needles, no "wait until I finish this row." It seemed a little too quiet, even with the sound of the TV in the background.

"No more knitting . . . ever?" I asked.

"Ever," he said firmly.

"But why?" It came out like a wail.

"You were right." He turned up the volume on the TV. "Knitting is stressful."

I hate being right.

Now They Say Knitting Relieves Stress

L. S. Rowe

"I have good news!" Tom said on the phone. I could tell from the traffic noise that he was on the road. That meant he was on the road driving to Ann Arbor from his home in Flint, sixty miles away. It was my favorite sound in the world.

"We're going to see Douglas Adams!" I yelled. I'd heard that the English humorist, author of *The Hitchhiker's Guide to the Galaxy*, which I'd loved since high school, was speaking that night at the Michigan Union, and that the event was sold out. But Tom had a magical way of making things happen, and he loved surprising people.

"Well, I am," Tom said, with less enthusiasm. His brother Paul had bought tickets for Tom and several other friends, but not for me. "But you'll get to see me later."

This was "good news"—that I'd see my boyfriend after he'd been doing the thing I wanted to do without me? It wasn't the first time Paul had deliberately excluded me, and it wouldn't be the last. After the ensuing fight, Tom called me back in a huff to tell me that he was going home and that Paul was angry at me for spoiling *his* evening. For a few minutes, the hurt was so great that I thought about suicide.

Tom wasn't the only problem. I'd been under intense stress, trying to hold down a full-time job and finish an architecture degree. I was living with a bitter and irritable girl, who I couldn't stand being around, and dating an alcoholic thirteen years older than myself. Add to that, I'd suffered from depression, mostly untreated, since childhood, and I was well on my way into a major episode.

As I sat on the kitchen floor in my second-story apartment, my limbs leaden with discouragement and my face red and tear-streaked, I imagined jumping off the balcony off the living room behind me. I imagined the pain of the landing and the possible broken limbs—lying on the cold, wet, early spring ground, not dead or dying, but unable to walk or move. I looked across the hallway to the tub in the bathroom. I didn't have any pills in the medicine cabinet that would do any good. I imagined myself lying in the tub, razor blade in my hand—but I didn't have any razor blades, and my X-Acto knives were at school, and all the kitchen knives were impossibly dull. I wanted to skip the pain step anyway. How could I end up in the hospital, so that someone else would have to take care of me and I wouldn't have to think or make any decisions anymore?

"God help me," I whispered, not sure if I was swearing or praying.

I needed to get out of the apartment, I realized. I needed a distraction. I called a friend who came and took me to Ashley's, an English-style pub near the university campus. We'd been there for a while, drinking hard cider from pint glasses, and I was feeling much less self-destructive, when in walked Douglas Adams himself!

He sat down at a table near ours with two younger people, probably the organizers of his speaking engagement.

It took another pint of cider and the encouragement of my companions, but I finally managed to suck it up and walk over to him, my knees like jelly, to tell him how much I liked his work and how disappointed I was not to have heard him speak, and could I please have his autograph? Graciously, he agreed. I had him make it out to Tom.

It still amazes me: on that darkest night of my life, God gave me the last laugh. Paul didn't meet Mr. Adams; Tom didn't see him; but I got to shake his hand and get his autograph!

During the days after the Douglas Adams incident, I went to a psychiatrist who prescribed medication that turned me into a vegetable. The therapist he referred me to told me that my problem was "performance anxiety." I sat on the couch for the next two weeks doing nothing but eating, smoking, and watching television. Being unable to function made me feel guilty, which didn't help. Then I remembered the unfinished knit sweaters in my closet—projects I'd started before the whirl of the college social scene and the pressures of classes had absorbed all my free time. I pulled out a sweater and started working on it. I stopped taking the medication because I didn't like being a vegetable. I lost my job. I kept knitting. I finished that first sweater and started working on the second. Tom and I made up. I kept knitting. I failed half my classes that semester, but that was okay because I was knitting. I moved out of my apartment and back home with my family, still knitting. I finished the second sweater and shopped for yarn for the next project. One Sunday afternoon, my sister let slip that the bitter ex-roommate had called to tell my mother about everything I'd done wrong because "I just thought you should know what Lisa's been up to, Mrs. Gillespie."

"We weren't going to tell you," my mother said. "We thought it was better just to let it go." I took a deep breath and kept knitting. She was right, and she very kindly never brought up anything my ex-roommate had told her.

I got engaged to Tom, but we broke up at Thanksgiving, when Paul specifically banned me from attending his wedding, where Tom was to be best man. By then I'd been in therapy for nine months *and* I had my knitting.

The repetitive clicks of the needles and the yarn sliding through my fingers soothed me as no medication ever could. I kept going to therapy—but I kept knitting too. It's entirely possible that the knitting kept me alive long enough for the therapy to get a chance to work. I loved seeing a finished project being worn, by me or someone else. I started to plan and make sweaters as gifts for close friends and family. I found that it is impossible to consider suicide when you have a project on the needles that you really want to see done and given away—especially when you also have a little ADD problem that keeps you starting new projects before the old ones are finished. I've since read articles in knitting magazines that say that scientists have discovered the therapeutic power of yarn and needles. I could have told them that years ago.

I moved to Chicago and worked as an architect for two years, knitting all the while. Eventually I decided to go back to school to finish that degree. Having learned that I'd rather be home knitting in my off hours instead of out socializing, school was much easier this time around.

Early in the spring, right before I graduated, Douglas Adams came to Ann Arbor for another speaking engagement, this time at the historic Michigan Theater. I was thrilled to be able to go with my friend Steve, who is now my husband. Afterward, we went to Ashley's, a nice celebration of how far I'd come.

We were drinking hard cider out of pint glasses when in walked Paul and some friends, who'd been at the event. Steve invited them to join us, and they pulled up chairs and started to gab as though it was the most natural gathering of friends in the world. I smiled and was polite and thought about my knitting. As we got up to leave, Paul turned to me and said, "Does that finally make up for last time?" It took every fiber of my Christian charity not to pick up the pitcher sitting in front of him and dump the contents over his head. I said nothing, turned, and left.

"Boy, he can be a jerk sometimes," Steve said as we walked out into the chilly air, slipping his hand into mine for comfort. "Are you okay?"

"I will be," I replied. I knew I would be, and I was. I went home to my knitting.

Knit Two Together: Friends

The Knitter's Imperative

Martha Hesselein

I met Evelyn because we had our radiation treatments at the same time every weekday at the Cancer Center. Her breast cancer from five years earlier had come back in her lung and bones. I was on my first round, hoping I wasn't seeing my future in the frail people with whom I shared the waiting room.

Every day I brought my knitting, a toe-up sock in Regia on size 1 double-pointed needles, to work on while I waited my turn. Soothing, undemanding: my recent chemotherapy left me with the dreaded "chemo brain," making concentration difficult. I was still bald from chemo but was the only woman at the Cancer Center at that time who didn't wear a wig, hat, or scarf. I got all the usual questions directed at public knitters— "Are you using toothpicks for that?" "Now, is that knitting or crochet?" The unspoken question was "Why the heck aren't you making yourself a hat?"

But Evelyn, on the first day, saw what I was doing and said, "I used to knit when I lived in New York." We bonded over comparing cancer treatments, talking about our young children, and sharing knitting stories. The next week she said, "I think I'll knit a hat for my niece's baby-to-be." I heard through the knitting grapevine that she visited our local yarn store that very day, oxygen tank in tow, to pick out yarns and needles. She already had an old pattern she wanted to use.

I saw the beginning of the hat the next week. She was on pain medications that made it difficult to think straight and she hadn't knit for years, but she had decided to make this hat and nothing was going to stop her. She handed me her knitting as soon as she arrived and said, "Figure out why this isn't working, will you?" and so I did as she went in for her dose of radiation. I frogged a bit and corrected the error. The hat pattern was not my idea of fun. I like hats that start at the bottom and get smaller with a minimum of fuss. I was known as the "fruit cap" lady several years back, and for good reason. This hat pattern was the sort I detest: knit back and forth, with a seam, crocheted edges, sewn-down facing, braided ties to gather the top, a garter stitch band under the chin, and a button. I don't see how it could have been any more complicated. And the yarn was cotton. I don't like cotton's lack of resilience and I refuse to be beguiled by its softness. And I didn't care for the colors—sand and sage. I was glad to be only helping a little, not actually making this hat.

Soon Evelyn's radiation treatments were stopped; they couldn't shrink the tumor that was causing her pain. I went to see her at her home. The pretense was to help her with knitting the hat, but we wanted to see each other and both felt a little shy outside of our usual meeting place in the Cancer Center waiting room. She hadn't made much progress on the hat and needed a few errors corrected. So I frogged and then reknit and we talked about our lives and how she was dying and how her kids felt about that. I made some progress and she got tired.

The last time I saw her alive, a few weeks later, she knew she would soon die. She had moved into a friend's house with a view over a little branch of the river. She told me she wanted me to finish the hat and send it to her niece. I said sure, thinking it must be almost done by now. How gracious I would be, putting the crochet edging on the little hat and sending it off with a modest yet charming note. She gave me a bag with the obnoxious cotton yarn, the fusty pattern and her wooden needles.

I smiled. "Where's the hat?" I asked.

"It was wrong, so I had to take it all out. You need to start over."

My gracious smile froze. "Okay."

"And I need you to make a matching sweater. I'll give you the yarn later. It's here somewhere but I can't find it."

The rest of my body froze—a whole sweater out of that stringy stuff? What could I say? "Okay."

I worked on the hat at her memorial service. I decided the hat (and soon the sweater) must be a penance for some knitting cruelty I had inflicted on someone in a previous life. I found the pregnant niece after the service and showed her the pattern and the half-finished hat. Her brow puckered as she looked at it and said, "Oh! You don't have to finish it." But of course I had to finish. I've never seen it written down, never heard it spoken, but I am positive there is a knitting imperative that goes like this: if a dying knitter gives you something to finish, you do it. By the time I finished that stupid hat, I hated it. But I also hated to let it go because it was my only link to my friend Evelyn.

I pray for her and for all those who have lost the fight. But I also pray that her family never finds the yarn for the sweater.

A Knitting Circle

Susan Gordon Lydon

Let's begin with circles.

Black Elk, the Oglala Sioux holy man, said long ago, "Everything an Indian does is in a circle, and that is because the power of the world always works in circles, and everything tries to be round. Even the seasons form a great circle in their changing, and always come back again to where they were. The life of a man is a circle from childhood to childhood, and so it is in everything where power moves."

Probably since the beginning of time, women have worked on handcrafts together in groups. In the nineteenth and early part of the twentieth centuries, quilting bees were a popular form of communal work and socializing for women. In a quilting bee, women together were able to accomplish a large task that one or two could not quickly do alone. In addition, almost all written accounts of American Indian life include scenes of women bent over their beadwork, visiting and advising one another as they work.

Once, on a trip to Canada, I came across a group in a small Ontario town who had been meeting weekly for years to make hooked rugs. They made fashioned kind of rug: you draw a picture on burlap an use different colored strips torn from worn-out woolen ing to form the pattern. The women, who were advance years, were happy to call themselves The Happy Hookers Strippers. But they had a serious purpose that went beyo the practice of craft: They had been together for so lon more than two decades, that they functioned as a suppor group. When one woman suffered a stroke, the other women finished her rug for her; they also brought her food and made sure she was comfortable. I asked the group if they told one another everything. "Not everything," one woman answered. "But a lot."

In the past few years, as knitting has regained popularity and expanded to include a younger generation, more and more women have begun to form knitting circles. Perhaps these groups take the place of the book clubs that started up a few years ago or the consciousness-raising groups of the early days of the women's movement. The value of female companionship, the practical help for problems, and the deep, quiet communion that take place all make knitting circles an increasingly attractive way for women to spend their time.

I had heard about knitting circles but hadn't encountered one myself until July of 2001. For the past few years I had been leading a spiritual knitting retreat at Esalen Institute in Big Sur in California. That July, six of the eight women who came to the retreat belonged to a group who call themselves a Stitch 'n' Bitch Club. They buy their yarn from L'Atelier in Los Angeles and meet together on Monday nights. I had been nervous before the workshop started, like a hostess who is

worried that no one will come to her party. When the women arrived on Friday night toting baskets and shopping bags spilling yarn, blankets, and sections of sweaters, I could have jumped for joy.

Several women were beginning knitters. Their enthusiasm was contagious and showed itself in exuberant innovations. They used imaginative color combinations, or invented new ways of making fringe, or worked yarns of seemingly incompatible gauges in different directions. I was so moved by their experiments that I hesitated to teach them conventional techniques. One beginner, Alex, became so enamored of knitting that she taught her mother, Ann, and two sisters to knit and invited them to join the Stitch 'n' Bitch. Lori, the most accomplished and experienced knitter, helped the newer knitters with their projects and problems. Another member, Zanny, didn't knit, but balled yarn for the knitters. One group member, Betsyann, recorded a CD of her sophisticated renditions of Frank Sinatra songs, called *Can I Be Frank?* When she performed in L.A. to celebrate the CD's release, the entire Stitch 'n' Bitch group showed up to support her.

These women were bonded. Several worked in the same industry, producing, casting, and directing commercials for television. But there was none of the hierarchical posturing or exclusivity I might have expected them to demonstrate. They seemed to possess a great feeling of equality and good fellowship, which they extended to the other two women in the retreat and the workshop leader, me.

Our workshop sessions were a mixture of silent knitting and meditation, coupled with deep sharing about our own life experience. As the weekend went on, the silences deepened,

taking on a richer quality, and the group seemed to coalesce into something solid, powerful, and even transcendent. By the end of our last session, all of us were exhilarated.

The younger women—in their twenties and early thirties—asked Ann, Alex's mother, and me about the women's movement. They wanted to know why our generation of feminists had devalued "women's work" such as keeping house or being a stay-at-home mother. During the early days of women's liberation, I had diverged from the general agenda of my group by wanting to explore the essential nature of being a woman, neither the imitation of men nor the socialized female role, but the true, internal meaning of female gender identity. Thirty years later, the deep discussions in this retreat group reminded me of the dreams I had had in those long-ago days. This younger generation did not have to decide between "women's work" and work in the world. They had choices, and the decision to take one path did not diminish the value of others. Talking with this group, I felt like I had come full circle.

Mac

Margaret Klein Wilson

If you'd said "llama" to me five years ago, the word would have conjured up images of a foreign pack animal, perhaps trekking along New England's forested mountain trails and ferrying in the picnics of urban day hikers. Or it might summon up the picturesque, well-groomed living lawn ornaments of budding gentleman farmers.

My limited knowledge of this cousin-to-a-camel was soon to change. I was about to become a shepherd again after a three-year hiatus from keeping sheep. Through a series of miracles, friends, and fate, my merino sheep and I were to live on a large farm with abundant fields, good barn space for my (now small) flock, and a welcoming house and studio space for me.

The single drawback to this arrangement was that I would be living almost half a mile from where the animals would be kept and pastured. A sizable population of foxes, fishers, and coyotes roamed the woods, wetland, and fields in between.

I needed a reliable guard animal to tend the sheep, without offending the walkers and joggers who also enjoyed this pleasant country road. A barking guard dog would be intimidating, a donkey too noisy and independent, and a permanent electrified fence was too expensive.

"Have you considered getting a llama?" asked a fellow shepherd. And so I set out to visit a llama-breeding farm in southwestern Vermont. Six hours and thirty close encounters-of-the-llama-kind later, I was cautiously smitten by Fleetwood Mac, a six-foot tall vegetarian with brown eyes you could swim in and a cocoa-colored wooly fleece that was a fiber lover's dream. His serene nature and energetic prance made him stately in a camelid kind of way. But, "Make no mistake," his breeder assured me. The merest hint of canine misbehavior would almost certainly trigger Mac's aggressive guarding behavior.

Mac was not fond of being touched, but after a few successful "catch and haltering" practices, my anxiety about handling him segued into confidence that we might be a good team. I signed on the dotted line and arranged a delivery date.

After living without my sheep for three years, the euphoria of setting up "farm" again soon became tinged with trepidation and buyer's remorse. What was I thinking? Keeping sheep was hard enough, but here I was taking on an expensive guard animal on faith. Would the llama do *his* work? Was this *my* right work?

Mac was delivered to the farm on the same cloudy November day my eight sheep arrived. Mac's entrance was auspicious. Unfolding himself from the back of the pickup truck, he stood tall, scoping out the barnyard with proprietary calm.

The correct way to greet a llama is to clasp your hands behind your back and lean forward, to gauge the limit of his personal space. I did. Unblinking, Mac looked me square in the eye, stretched forward and granted me a gentle but inquisitive sniff on my forehead. Nose to nose, we sized each other up. I was mesmerized by his huge intelligent eyes, extraordinary eyelashes, velvety muzzle, and unabashed curiosity. His long rabbitlike ears flicked comically as he studied me likewise.

We took a stroll along the paddock driveway, me giving him plenty of rope, he not taking advantage of a loose lead line and my tentative regard. Equal partners. His response to everything he encountered was gentle but assured. So far, so good.

Tucking him into the stall with the sheep for the evening, I watched them shuffle around each other with startled curiosity. I fervently hoped for an easy bonding and for Mac's guarding instinct to click into gear. He had never even seen sheep! Faced with a coyote or an aggressive dog, could pure instinct really provoke an effective response?

"Reading" Mac's behavior for evidence of his guarding instinct became the neighborhood pastime. The phone began ringing with Mac stories. My neighbors Barbara and Roy reported the details of their first Mac visit. Sure enough, as they approached the fence that first day, Mac planted himself between them and the flock. "Yup," crowed Roy, "he's gonna guard all right."

And Mac did. He gave every passing dog the evil eye. At the least sign of anything out of order, including me wearing sunglasses or a new hat, Mac herded the sheep into the barn. Visitors bearing carrots were treated with a slightly goofy but beneficent deference. Discriminating and dutiful, he assumed the role of bouncer and butler without missing a beat.

In early December, the weather turned sharply cold and windy overnight. One morning, I entered the paddock through the lower gate, pulling it shut but not hitching it closed. I'd be leaving that way soon. First, I enjoyed the simple pleasure of my work—feeding out good hay to the sheep, energetic and hungry on a bitter morning. Mac, however, was humming with concern around my oldest sheep, Belle. Frail and beloved, she was suffering from the abruptness of this cold snap.

There is always a moment that anyone who keeps animals experiences when they add a new animal to their life. That moment when suddenly you understand they have become firmly woven into your heart and life. Right then, watching Mac buffer Belle from the push and shove of the morning feeding frenzy, I felt my heart open. I had come to simply adore this solicitous good-natured beast.

I had to make a decision on Belle's behalf immediately. Quite upset, I left the barn by a different gate to think through the options and then consult the vet. Not long after, a neighbor was pounding on my front door: "The llama is loose and running this way!"

I jumped into the car nearly in tears. The prospect of losing two animals in one day was unbearable. How do you catch a llama on the run? If he went too far, how would he find home again? I drove toward the farm and there was Mac, running in my direction in the field alongside the road.

Was this dumb luck or did he understand this was the direction I approached the barn from, twice a day? I jammed on the brakes, rolled down the window and shouted. He stopped. We took a long look at each other and then I started driving to the barn, praying he would follow.

In a moment worthy of a *National Geographic* special, Mac spun around and kept pace with me, floating along in a determined gallop, neck outstretched and eyes dead ahead, right up to the wide-open gate swinging in the wind. We stepped into the paddock, Mac snorting as if in reprimand, and then high-stepping his way up to the barn to count our sheep. At that moment I was sure of two things: Mac had intentionally fetched me to close the gate; and for that, I loved him absolutely.

One evening not long after, I arrived at the barn after a powdery snowfall, looking forward to chores and checking on Belle's recovery. The sky was inky blue, the air soft and still. Mac wafted down to the gate in the pale night to escort me up to the barn and the sheep.

I always enjoyed this nightly ritual, and tonight, the snow and peace added to the pleasure. Following Mac, tracing his deliberate steps with my own, I realized his path was not a straight line from point A to B, but a pleasing forty paces of serpentine, meandering grace. Mac not only knew his work, he delighted in it: a gentleman of a guard and a poet as well.

Elana

Kathryn Tewson

Elana and I broke up eight and a half years ago. From that sentence, you'd think we were dating, but while our relationship was as emotionally intimate and bitterly dysfunctional as any marriage, it was never physical. She had graduated from the same college I had flunked out of, and we decided it would be fun for her to drive across the country and come live with me.

Elana is an amazing knitter, the kind of technical artist who can produce a sweater out of string and air with no real pattern or sense of direction. At the time, she knit exclusively on straight needles, stubbornly refused to check gauge, and didn't finish the collars of her sweaters because she and circular needles didn't get along. She could crochet a baby bootie in the time it took me to smoke a cigarette, which I promised her the day we signed the lease that I would never do in the apartment. She liked fast motorcycles and loud music. I found her once on a bar stool in a punk club knitting savagely away on an intricately cabled sweater from heavy Irish wool, with paper napkins shoved into one nostril of her mosh-pit-induced bloody nose to keep the blood off the work.

At the time, I neither knit nor crocheted. I didn't do much

of anything, in fact. I was in the grips of a crushing depression, and I envied Elana her ability to cook a meal, hold a job, balance a checkbook, clean the house and, yes, knit.

After about a year, unfortunately, my black depression and her savage temper ran amuck with each other, and our friendship collapsed in ruins. She threw a pot at my head and threatened to follow it with a knife; I left the apartment and hid at my boyfriend's for two weeks. When I came back, a blanket of mold had settled over the dirty dishes in the sink, all the furniture was gone, and there was a pay or vacate notice pinned to the door.

Elana and I did not speak for seven years. During that time, I gradually scraped my life off the asphalt; I got a job I could hold, found a therapist I could trust, and made a home with my boyfriend. We bought a house. We planned to get married. I learned to knit. And every time I chopped garlic or made rice pudding or cast on for a project, I thought of Elana and wondered how she was doing, and if she still hated me.

About six weeks before my wedding, a mutual friend of ours reintroduced us over email. (He had no idea of our history—he just thought we'd get along well.) After a few cautious emails and false starts, Elana and I agreed to meet for lunch.

I was sick with worry and fear. I left my house far too early, drove far too fast, and ended up at the restaurant an hour ahead of time. After about four minutes of pacing, I got back in the car, headed to a nearby yarn shop, and picked up some more size 1 needles and some hand-dyed sock yarn in cotton-candy colors. I went back to the restaurant and cast on my sock, staring blankly off into space and trying not to think too hard while my hands made K1P1 ribbing on the tiny needles with the fine, fine wool. With every knit stitch, I'd think "It will be fine." With every purl stitch, I'd think "Please don't hate me." In that Zen focus space, I drank my coffee and waited for my once and future friend to arrive.

When she sat down across from me, her first words were, "OH THANK GOD you're knitting! That means I can knit too!" Her second words were "Man those are tiny little needles. Whatcha makin?"

"Socks," I said.

And I swear to God, her eyes got wide and she said, "Oh, my GOD, Kathryn, I've wanted to make socks my whole life but I could never figure it out! Oh, will you teach me how to make socks? Please?"

"Sure," I said, grinning. "So how've you been?"

An hour and a half later, we left the restaurant and went back to the yarn shop, where I set her up with some size 4 double points and some superwash worsted wool yarn. We parked ourselves in the back corner, and I taught Elana how to make socks. When I showed her how to join the stitches by swapping the first and last stitch on the needles, she squealed with delight and said "That's so PUNK!" in a voice loud enough to be heard throughout the store. She insisted that size 4 needles were quite small enough for her, thank you very much, and that you'd never catch her knitting on those teeny little toothpicks. By the time the yarn shop employees apologetically told us that we had to get out—they'd turned off the lights in the hope that we'd get the hint but it just wasn't taking—Elana had started the heel of her first sock.

It's been more than a year, now, and Elana and I are fast friends again, only more honest and less crazy. We both knit socks obsessively; Elana described hand-knit wool socks to a stranger as "just like falling in love, only quieter." She confessed to me that when she left the apartment, she stole my copy of *Joy of Cooking* to vent her anger on me so she didn't have to set all my stuff on fire; I confessed to her that I used to smoke in the apartment all the time.

Last weekend, she bought her first set of size 0 double points. I think this could be the start of a beautiful friendship.

Susan

Peggy Neuber

To tell you the truth, I always envied Susan a little. In fact, I coveted Susan's life with its air of graciousness and calm. Susan chose not to have kids, and I have two and while there has been endless joy in being a parent, there also have been chaos, disrupted plans, dreams put on hold, and a very cluttered house. Well, that's not quite fair—a good percentage of the clutter is my stuff, including a basement with thirteen boxes of yarn sorted according to color and fiber type. In contrast, Susan's house was a study in order and tastefulness. She never kept things she didn't use and what she did have was clean and well kept. Take her closet, for instance. She had two or three skirts, five or six blouses, maybe three pairs of shoes, one pair of jeans and a few sweaters, mostly hand knit. That was it. She wasn't one to hang on to clothes she'd outgrown in hopes of shrinking back to a smaller size one day. Unlike me, she didn't go to the thrift shop and end up bringing home yet one more tie-dyed T-shirt to add to my collection of five that I hardly wear. Her kitchen had just enough dishes, all lovely antiques and not even one plastic cup from a fast food outlet. She was the type to have one perfect flower in a crystal vase on the un-smudged wood table. We had dinner there once and even the food was a work of art—we had a beet salad that was almost too beautiful to eat. Let's just say that she probably never made fluorescent orange mac and cheese from a box. She worked hard at keeping her life calm, simple, and orderly. Her house and life were works of art.

I had met Susan in a women's journal group. A group of about twelve women came together once a week to share their writings about their lives. As a result, we grew very close over the years. As with other aspects of her life, Susan's writing was poetic and artful. I have to admit that sometimes I didn't understand what she was trying to say, but she never complained about her husband and kids and her messy house. She would write about enjoying a single red geranium on a windowsill while I would write about trying to find a babysitter after my last one moved. Even her penmanship was flowing and straight, with no scratched-out words or indecipherable writing.

We were so different, it's a wonder we became friends at all, but we did. One of the things we liked to do together was talk about what we were knitting or spend an afternoon drinking tea and knitting together. Susan actually finished projects, usually from her own lovely handspun yarn. She didn't buy more fleeces or roving until she had spun and used the yarn from what she had. I liked to call Susan when I was feeling frustrated or blue because she was a good listener. In one of these telephone conversations, I began to sense that she wasn't very happy in her marriage. It wasn't more than a year later that she separated from her husband and filed for divorce. About that time she stopped coming to journal group too. Maybe the intimacy made her uncomfortable.

Some months later, I found out that she had been diagnosed with ovarian cancer, a very lethal type. Now it was my turn to be a listener and to help this friend who always seemed so capable and independent. She had surgery followed by the usual rounds of chemotherapy, which made her long blond hair fall out. Even with a bald head, she was graceful and stately. She took to wearing a fleece hat but never resorted to a wig. The chemotherapy held the cancer at bay for a while, but eventually, it moved to her liver and she agreed to a stem-cell replacement as a last resort. This is a very costly procedure that her insurance company denied because it seldom works on ovarian cancers. Her many friends held a fundraiser and amazingly, we raised the entire $90,000.

Before she left for the hospital, eighty-six miles away, for the treatment, I asked her if I could bring her anything to take with her since her recovery would be several weeks. I brought her a pair of tweedy wool socks I had knit to keep her feet warm in the hospital. She wanted her own knitting project, so I bought her some cheerful colorful sock yarn and nice bamboo needles and provided my favorite basic sock pattern.

After a period of quarantine, she finally came back to town and I called to see how she was feeling and how the socks were coming. She told me she had taken out the ribbing several times because of mistakes, but finally had knit down to turning the heel and needed my help. I invited her for one of our tea and knitting afternoons. She took off her fleece hat as she came through my front door and I was overjoyed to see that her hair had grown back, this time into brown shiny curls. She joked that it was her $90,000 hairdo. We sat down on the futon in the curtain-filtered afternoon sun and knitted awhile, but she seemed tired and frustrated with the project. After about an hour, she said that she was giving up on the sock, that it reminded her too much of the hospital, that she could even smell the hospital in the wool. She asked if I would take the one half sock and finish it along with the second. Of course, I secretly planned to finish them and present them back to her, but I was not quick enough.

Susan died a couple of months later, late July. Her sisters arranged for her friends to gather one more time in Susan's perfect house to hold a combination potluck wake and memory-sharing time. We sat among the flowers that she had planted that spring and watched the sun go down over the western mountains and felt our lovely Susan slipping away as surely as the sunlight.

That fall I finished the socks. The knitting was a catharsis of sorts for me. I knitted away my sadness and hurt at losing Susan. I realized that life is still for the living and the best memorial to anyone gone is to live your own life as if everything is a blessing and a miracle. I donated the socks to a fundraiser for our local Nature Center. Both Susan and I were credited in the program. Even after her death, her spirit was alive in those socks.

Someday I will join the eternal circle of knitters. I do hope Susan is saving a comfy chair and a hot cup of my favorite tea for me.

Eye of the Grouse

Jeannine Bakriges

The projects I knit from the yarn I spin and color with natural dyes are as much my personal signature as when I write my name with its own flourish. Ideas for fiber arts can vary from the in-your-face obvious to the unexpected and ethereal. I enjoy combining diverse elements. The components brew and simmer until a cohesive, if still somewhat tentative, design evolves. The process can take hours or years.

Sometimes I find inspiration in relationships, human or otherwise. Grouse entered my life as the latter. He arrived as southern Vermont's glorious autumnal colors were darkening to a damp, earthy brown. Out of the dense forest and marshy area below our yard, Grouse purposefully climbed. I was busily tending a pot of water filled with black walnut hulls. The rich liquid would dye lustrous, scoured Romney wool, destined for some skillful spinner's hands. Grouse sidled up to me and began earnestly chatting as if we were the oldest of friends. Clearly he did not believe that he was supposed to be a wild bird. At first I called him "Madame," but later apologized when a naturalist neighbor corrected me. He was a male ruffed grouse. After that, I simply called him Grouse.

From the start, as I went about my dyeing work, he would scurry to stay by my side, always talking nonstop. I knew without a doubt that a profound friendship was forming—the kind one didn't know one needed until it happened, but also the kind one never forgets.

Grouse would sometimes show up daily, but it wasn't unusual for a few weeks to go by between visits. He would generally stay for several hours. If I had to go inside, he would wait, disgruntled and impatient, by the door. He was truly a pitiable sight if he realized I was leaving in a car.

Grouse was cordial to visitors and would perch on their car like a welcoming ambassador. As time went on, he would crawl on my lap or climb to my shoulder, though I never attempted to touch him with my hands or make him a pet.

As the sun faded, Grouse would make his way down into the marsh, heading for deep forest. I'd wish him a fond farewell, always telling him to be wary of the predators who were sure to be lurking.

One crisp and sunny day, I was tending yet another dyepot, passing the time with my nose in a novel. Grouse arrived quietly and grazed on tender grass shoots near me. For the first time I became truly aware of the patchwork of patterns decorating his body. The colors varied, from satiny beiges and weathered rusts to saturated browns. Each section of his body boasted a delightfully different combination, showing off his intricately detailed feathers. Topping off all of this splendor was a flamboyant crown that Grouse raised or lowered according to reasons only he knew. I asked him to sit tight while I ran into the house to get my knitting idea notebook. He seemed pleased by the positive vibes exuding from me. I sketched the beautiful patterns and noted the color combos. As I looked into his eyes, I saw that they were the richest, most soulful brown of all—eyes that knew a forest I could never be part of. These were eyes and feathers beckoning to be handspun, hand-dyed, and hand-knitted.

Winter came and several months went by without a Grouse visit. Just as a spring snow blanketed my yard, he tapped his beak on my deck window. I ran out, happily proclaiming, "Grouse!" He was equally happy to see me, going by his chatter and his crown's frantic popping up and down. I saw him almost daily thereafter.

I wish I could give this true story a fairytale ending. I cannot. One terrible day Grouse showed up with an eye missing. He cried and I cried. He told me the story of the horrific event over and over. I gathered that the culprit was a fisher. I wrestled with the idea of building him a shelter and then thought otherwise. Grouse was wild, whether he knew it or not. Penning him up was not how he was meant to live out his life, especially with me as jailer. He would never have understood I aimed only to protect him. I did realize the bitter reality that we didn't have long together because his injury made him a very vulnerable target. He came back a few more times, but in the end he vanished.

Caring friends told me how some Native American tribes viewed animals who come to humans. Such an event is considered sacred and incredibly special. Celebratory dance and drumming are the hallmark of a grouse/human relationship. Grouse was a symbol that all human activity is a form of dance and ancient ritual. His visits represented dealing with change in a way that would allow a surge of positive energy to flow into my life. Grouse's memory lives on in my heart and in the knitting, based on my sketches of him, that I felt deeply honored to create.

Knitting a Prayer

Karna J. Converse

I could tell something was wrong as soon as I sat down on the bleachers next to Martha. Her eyes, usually bright, were dull and lifeless—sad enough to cry but too tired to put forth the effort. Her hair, usually chic and stylishly combed, framed her face like a black cloud of worries.

"I need your prayers," she said. "The kids and I moved out of the house this week." The bounce-bounce-swish of basketballs hitting the gym floor and sliding through the nets echoed in the background.

Most Saturdays, I knitted while my third-grader shot baskets. On this particular morning, I listened. Martha talked about her husband's drinking and yelling and how counseling wasn't working. Their problems had been going on for several years, she said, and she knew the situation wasn't going to change. The hardest thing, she added, was telling her five children, especially the two boys.

"I told them that part of my job is to make sure they know how to treat women, especially their wives. I finally had to tell them that the way their daddy was treating me was not the right way." I could only nod my head in support because other parents began joining us on the bleachers.

For the next hour, we cheered when our sons took a shot and smiled discreetly when they dribbled the ball off their feet. When the buzzer sounded, fifty red-faced, sweaty boys made their way to the bleachers. Our sons high-fived their good-byes. In the confusion of grabbing coats and handing out water bottles, I could only look Martha's way to say "good-bye" and "I'll be praying for you." She smiled a thank-you. Her eyes still weren't sparkling, but neither were they lifeless.

I slung my bag over my shoulder with a newfound interest in the project it held. The prayer shawl I was knitting, I decided, had to be for Martha.

I first met Martha four years ago, when our boys were playing T-ball, but our conversations never progressed past the polite hello. The boys attend different schools and churches and so, for several years, our paths seldom crossed. Last year, the boys were on the same baseball team; Martha and I became bleacher buddies. At one of the first games of the season, we sat on cold metal bleachers, wrapped head to foot in blankets and wondered aloud at the wisdom of playing Little League Baseball in May. Sometime during that game, the polite remarks made between two spectator-moms turned into genuine interest in each other as friends.

"I know you're Geoffrey's mom," she started, "but I can't remember your name."

"Oh, thank you," I said, "I know you're Dillon's mom, but I can't remember your name either."

It was a simple conversation, yet it invited me to her side for the season's twelve games. She reminisced about her children's younger years when I distributed quarters to mine for Laffy Taffy and Big Chew Bubblegum. I saw a glimpse of my future when she monitored her teenagers' whereabouts via cell phone. It seemed she had it all together. Happy. Energetic. Always ready with a hug or word of comfort for her children. We parted after the boys' last game, joking that our butts needed a couple of months to recover and promising to remember each other's names at the next set of bleachers.

In the meantime, I learned how to knit.

An announcement in our church newsletter read: "Knit one. Pray one. Help start our prayer shawl ministry. This ministry combines knitting with praying as you make a prayer shawl for someone in need. Ethel Johnson has offered to get people started and/or teach people how to knit." I was the first to sign up, though my reasons were more selfish than benevolent.

When my husband's grandmother tried to teach me a

couple of years ago, her fingers moved faster than her explanations and my fingers weren't coordinated enough to earn her respect. Knitting a prayer shawl, I thought, was the perfect way to prove I could do it. Ethel assured me I'd learn in no time.

"We'll start with this scrap yarn before we go to the good stuff," she said. "OK, now watch. Under the loop, around the needle, and back through the loop. Under, around, and back through. Under, around, through. Here, you try." I grasped the yarn and attempted to weave it around my fingers, but the yarn snagged and the needles dropped to my lap. Gradually my clumsiness disappeared and I completed twenty stitches. Just keep practicing, she said, and call me when you need help.

We talked several times over the next few weeks, but finally, I felt confident enough to start with the "good" yarn. It was a bigger project than I expected and it took all winter. I knitted while I waited for kids after school and in between conversations at basketball games. Martha monitored my progress every Saturday morning, marveling at how large the shawl was getting and how soft it felt.

The instructions suggested I weave a prayer into the shawl, but I had to concentrate on the "under, around, through" mantra. Instead of praying the words printed on the instruction sheet, I remembered the sadness in Martha's eyes and thought about her courage. I prayed for her safety and her happiness. I hoped my stitches stayed knitted, and the prayer shawl would be useful.

Six months after casting on my first stitch, I bound off my last. I knew it wasn't perfect, but Ethel was full of compliments.

"I can't believe how nice it looks," she gushed. "Whoever gets it won't notice that you added a few stitches. They'll appreciate your effort."

I hoped this was true. It had been more than two months since I'd seen Martha and I knew my bleacher buddy would be surprised to hear from me. There was a split-second hesitation in her response when I called. A smile that was welcoming, yet curious, when I walked into her kitchen. But the warmth in her eyes invited me to speak.

"It's not perfect," I began, "but I want you to have it." I pulled the prayer shawl from my bag and handed it to her. She smiled in recognition of what was once a purple mass of yarn and brushed aside my comments on its imperfections. She wrapped the shawl around herself, demonstrating her answer to Dillon's "What do you do with it?" Then he wrapped it around his shoulders and left in search of a mirror.

"Thank you," she said, reaching out to hug me. She released me with a half-embarrassed, half-nervous laugh. "I didn't realize you were so much taller than me. I must always wear heels or something."

"Either that, or we must never stand up." We scored a three-pointer with our joke. Her smile assured me that she appreciated the gift, no matter how the stitches looked. And her eyes? They glistened.

You Owe Me

Nilda Mesa

"They sold Le Fourmie d'Or."

It was the biggest news to hit Puy-de-Montremouche-de-Villefranche-sur-Mouton (pop. 346) since André Malraux picked neighboring Sarlat to beautify in the mid-1960s. Liz, divorced, fiftyish, British, and a real estate agent, was the first to relay the news to Wilson.

"They sold Le Fourmie d'Or," Wilson told Agnes, his wife, as he hung up the phone.

"Oh, no! Now where will we go to eat? I mean, L'Abeille Gaté is just not as good."

Every summer for the past twenty years, Wilson and Agnes escaped New York for Puy. In New York, Wilson wrote talk show gags and wore his shirts untucked, marking himself as a hipster while denying his paunch. Agnes was a catalog photographer with heavy black-rimmed glasses. At the medieval Dordogne village, they nurtured a summer colony of English-speaking artists, poets, and composers. All indulged their bucolic French fantasies at revolving dinner parties with endless bottles of Côtes du Rhone and *le bon cuisine perigordeux*.

Years before, the earliest anglaises bought rundown stone manoirs dirt cheap. As word got out about the Dordogne, prices went up, and the real Montremouchais bequeathed their houses and tragic memories of the Great War to pottery, ice cream, and Indian-cotton shops. The Montremouchais built new dry homes with central heating and tall refrigerators. Even the town grocer moved, leaving the one and only mediocre baker in the Dordogne.

"Liz says it's not a restaurant anymore, and the person who bought it is Scottish. Name is Chris."

"Man or woman?" asked Agnes.

"I think a man, but I'm not sure."

"Married? Single?"

"I dunno."

"Geez, you're supposed to find out," Agnes teased. "Well,

we should invite him or her or whatever over to welcome them."

One week later, a slightly balding Viking in a kilt turned up for dinner bearing a bottle of Bordeaux.

"Hi, I'm Chris. You must be Agnes."

"That's not a Scottish accent! Where are you from, Minnesota?" Agnes blushed. "Oh, I'm so sorry. Welcome, come on in."

Chris laughed. "How did you know? I was in Scotland the last thirty years—with all that's going on it's just easier to say I'm Scottish. And you don't sound like a New Yorker."

"Grew up in Iowa City. Here's Wilson." Wilson extended his hand from behind Agnes.

"Welcome. Nice outfit," he quipped.

"This is how you dress to go to someone's house for dinner in Scotland."

"But we're in France," deadpanned Wilson.

"Hey, I'm still learning."

Over the course of dinner, they learned that last year Chris's wife left him for his best friend. Liz and Chris were sleeping together but had no expectations. He worked on an oil rig off the coast of Scotland. He had bought the rustic old restaurant on an impulse on the way to Sarlat, trying to forget his old life while not deciding quite what to do with the new one. They traded stories about growing up in the Midwest, and the necessity of keeping a low profile as Americans in Europe. Agnes found him genial, earthy, and vulnerable, and immediately began thinking of a suitable match for him.

"Leave the poor guy alone," said Wilson. "He's licking his wounds. Liz is good for him for now."

Nonetheless, that winter back in New York, Agnes was delighted to get Chris's email that he'd started dating Elodie, the local yarn shop owner. Her shop was at the edge of town in the old mill, and it was Agnes's gossip-free haven. She and Elodie were the same age, and bonded over wool, stitch patterns, and knitting magazines. Elodie's relationships had been complicated and rapid since she left her son's father after too many broken plates and stitches. Agnes had wished Elodie's life would even out, and now Chris had come along.

"Well, that should help his French," Agnes told Wilson in their kitchen while sautéing leeks.

"Not necessarily. But maybe he'll get a good sweater for those long winter nights."

"Don't say that. Remember? If you knit your boyfriend a sweater you'll break up."

"So that's why I still haven't gotten a sweater." He winked. "Eh, they probably don't have the same curse in France. It's probably a different curse, like a food curse. I mean, you never see French guys wearing bad sweaters."

"That's just because we're never there in winter so we don't know. They're romantic enough that they probably would. And I'm working on your sweater, by the way. Yarn's wound off."

Through the winter, the emails kept coming, sometimes from Chris, sometimes with a note at the bottom from Elodie. Language didn't seem to be a barrier.

Until Chris came back from work in Scotland. Elodie had a new love. The emails blamed her, blamed him. No time for a sweater. Agnes felt vaguely guilty.

Not knowing what to say, Agnes asked Chris whether he saw knitting books in any bookstores in Scotland. She then emailed all her friends with UK connections that she was desperately seeking a Stella Moore book, which was fetching over $400 on eBay and Amazon. "Whoever sends me info leading to the purchase of *Colour Charts* will get a pair of handknit socks in their color of choice," she typed.

Chris fired off URLs to bookstores in Lerwick, Glasgow, and Edinburgh, hoping for his reward. The others said they'd never heard of the book.

That summer in Puy, Chris arrived in khakis for the annual summer kickoff dinner.

"That tramp," he said, downing a shot.

"We all tried to warn you," oozed Liz, rolling her eyes at Wilson. Agnes pressed her lips together.

"Hey, thanks for the wine, buddy," chirped Wilson.

That cracked the tension. The evening was raucous, witty and full of artichokes, hidden truffles, and wild strawberries with the Sauternes.

At the yarn store the next day, Agnes stroked the grey sock yarn, then the navy. But not at Elodie's. She found herself going there less often, telling herself that Elodie's business had picked up and she didn't want to distract Elodie from her customers.

"Grey or navy?" she asked Wilson.

"Why are you making him socks at all? He didn't get you the book, did he? Don't you have enough projects?" Wilson remembered his unfinished sweater.

The next time Agnes saw Chris on the street he bent down to kiss her cheek, lingered, and said warmly, "So when do I get my socks?"

Agnes lowered her eyes. "You didn't qualify. Remember, my offer was for info leading to the purchase of the book, and none of those bookstores had it." Agnes squinted into the sun so she wouldn't see his face.

"Aw, dammit! I was really looking forward to warm socks this winter."

"Geez, I'm sorry. I really appreciate the trouble you went to. But I wound up getting it at full price from this online bookstore in Oregon."

"You owe me." He looked directly in her eyes.

"Oh come on. Hey, why don't you come over for dinner Thursday—my friend Judith is visiting and we need another male to round out the party."

"Is she cute?"

"She's going through a nasty divorce and she's not ready. Besides she lives in New York. She's a lawyer."

"Kids?"

"No. Weimaraners. Now that's enough. Can you make it?" Agnes asked sweetly.

"Sure. It's not like my telephone's been ringing off the hook," he grumbled.

After dinner Chris invited Judith back for a nightcap. They both overlooked it every time he called her Agnes. Judith said he made her feel alive again. In town, Chris couldn't keep his hands off her. At dinner parties, Liz and Judith baited each other on colonialism. Liz baited Agnes on American prudishness over extramarital affairs. Agnes told Judith she was happy for her. Elodie never came up.

Suddenly it was over. Chris looked sullen and began leaving out cases of empty wine bottles on trash day. "I told you she wasn't ready," offered Agnes.

"You owe me."

That winter Chris sold the house to Au Foie Brulé, a chain of paté stores, and moved to Normandy. He never called Wilson back the next summer. Agnes learned to spin.

In Memory Of

Cheryl Murray

I will choose blue yarn. John's eyes were blue and it was his favorite color. He was fourteen and he died recently.

I never knew John, but years ago I loved his father. We were together a long time, but I never knit anything for him. I don't believe in the "boyfriend sweater curse," but I think I subconsciously knew that this wasn't a forever romance, one worthy of knitted gifts.

We separated, moved to different cities, married other people, and became caught up in life's flow. For over twenty years we've maintained a connection from our shared pasts—a connection as fragile, yet resilient, as cobweb lace yarn.

From 1,500 miles away I grieve for his loss and wish I could do something—anything—to help.

Of course, knitters have always known what to do in this situation—they knit something. It is time, at last, to knit something for John's father.

A scarf to hug his neck and warm his heart. Blue yarn. Very, very soft.

Three ribs flank a center cable motif. Three is a powerful number: father, mother, child; Holy Trinity; past, present, future. The cable itself is a simple rope cable crossing around itself fourteen times to symbolize the years that John's life intertwined with ours. Then the cable will split and continue as two separate bars to show how our paths will continue moving ahead through time, in the same direction, but independently. The open area between the legs stands for the empty space that John's death leaves in our lives. Finally, the cable will rejoin as a reminder of the hope that someday John and his father will be reunited.

This scarf does not exist yet, except in my imagination. But by simply knitting it in my head it is already real to me. It comforts me to picture my fingers making the stitches that represent a life and with each stitch I send out prayers of protection for my own child.

If John's father finds as much comfort in the wearing of this scarf as I will in the knitting, it will serve us both well.

In Which It Is Discovered That I Am Not Ann Patchett

Ann Shayne

I'm walking down a leafy side street in Manhattan, looking for the townhouse of a woman I've never met. She's hosting a party for people she's never met, and the people at the party have never met each other either. I'm wondering if I'm wearing the proper shoes, the ones that define Me. I realize in a panic that I have failed to wear any handknits.

I'm beginning to remember that the house number matters a lot in New York City. How could I forget to write down the address? Back home in Nashville, you can often wing it: drive down a street, see a bunch of cars, and conclude that your party is right there. A row of New York townhouses gives you no help at all. It's 113 or 131 or 115, and they all look likely. I dig in my purse for my phone. I'm calling Kay, who's sitting in that townhouse waiting for me to show up.

I've come a thousand miles to sew up charity blankets, but mostly I've come to meet Kay. Meeting Kay has taken on the urgency of a trip to meet the future in-laws. "Have you met Kay yet?" "When are you going to meet?" "*Are* you going to meet?" "Don't you think it's weird that you've never even met Kay?" At this point people ask me about Kay the way I ask my son about his imaginary friend. *It may be that Ann is making all this up*. I can tell they are thinking this. *Maybe she needs to get out a little more*.

My friends are relieved that I'm going to New York. My conspiracy-theory friend Katie hopes something sinister will come of it, that Kay is a stalker or that she's really a twelve-year-old boy. Frannie hopes that Kay is actually nice and not just sort of nice. What they forget is that I've known Kay for a long time and she knows a lot about me. We're real, all right: you can't fake the complaints of a stay-at-home mother.

It began three years ago, when I posted my first-ever message on an Internet website. I was knitting a Rowan Yarns pattern. (It was Deco, from Rowan Number 29, a summer cardigan in a dreamy yarn called Linen Drape. It had a silvery sleekness to it and a lack of buttons.) Deco wasn't going well. Because my yarn store lacked Linen Drape, and because I was too dumb to know better, and because Hubbo was with me at the store (he accepts the blame), I substituted the dreadfully inappropriate NorskyDorsky ZooperTweed in not-sleek shades of lapis lazuli and kelly green. The gauge went wonky, the yarn displayed Failure to Drape, and I was making it in a size that would have fit Mr. Puffy The Marshmallow Man. In my frustration I went to the Rowan Yarns website. They have a special message board for subscribers to their magazine. I screwed up the nerve to post a message about this doomed project. I said I was "stewing" over this pattern, which conveyed an iota of my irritation. Somebody named Kay Gardiner responded, saying she was having problems with Deco. Her sleeves were too long. She might as well have said, "I am your long-lost sister" or "I have the snakebite kit right here."

The Rowan message board is a place where you can start to feel really chummy with people, mostly British, who share your unholy love of high-end yarn. You can throw a word like *gobsmacked* in there and nobody blinks. You are identified by your real name, first and last—it's all very straightforward and proper, with nobody named knitho or iluvyarnz266 or krabbyknitter. No email addresses are shown. I was fascinated by this online Biosphere where there was no such thing as too much knitting.

After a few weeks, Kay disappeared from the Rowan message board. I happened to have the email address of exactly one Rowanette, the spectacular sock knitter Polly who, in addition to copious knitting, liked to organize worldwide knitting exchanges involving dozens of knitters who didn't know each other. Polly knew all. I asked what had happened to Kay. "Daughter is very sick, in the hospital for two weeks," was the response.

I was stunned. This was my first experience with what we later came to call the Tip of the Iceberg Syndrome, which happens a lot online. As long as the talk is about knitting, everybody is on the same page. But that slim overlap on the Venn Diagram, that sliver called Knitting Obsession, leaves a lot of room for illness, sadness, crabbiness, bad taste, and embarrassing hobbies. You can be chirpy for exactly as long as it takes to write an email, then return to the murky parts of your life that nobody online can see.

Unless, of course, you decide to write about them. When I read that Kay's nameless daughter was sick, I asked Polly for Kay's email address. When Kay wrote back to me about her daughter's unexpected, terrifying illness, I instantly wrote back about my own brush with sick family. Just like that, I let it fly. We moved through the perils of staying home with children after loving your career (How Not to Feel Like a Freeloader? It's Impossible!), the merits of Jackson Browne (Kay stands firm, I waver), and the large and prickly topic of marriage. (When your husband leaves three months' worth of *Barrons* on the floor, do you pick it up or not?) We found endless things in common—Jewish husbands, two kids, fast typing, ownership of the same kind of SUV, encyclopedic knowledge of Patsy Cline lyrics, a morbid fear of things that smell bad. We weren't Internet pals, we were freaky Internet twins. I was curious to see how much I could learn about Kay simply by writing to her, and I was surprised that I wanted to tell her about my life. It seemed antiquated to have a correspondent, even if the correspondent was corresponding on a computer hooked up to the Internet. At many moments I thought it would be easier to pick up the phone, but I feared the spell would break and she would sound like some character from *Fargo*, or she would discover just how superfakeynice I really am.

Our Thelma-and-Louise-drive-the-car-over-the-cliff moment of true friendship came after about a year of emails.

Shameless eBay hounds, we both noticed a sizeable lot of old knitting books up for auction. It was the mother lode, the last great undisturbed stash of Rowanalia, being deaccessioned by an actual lady in Yorkshire, the home turf of Rowan Yarns—the provenance, the provenance! Great flopping intarsia sweaters from the '80s, models with hair as big as South Dakota, many styles of hot pants to ponder—we could complete our collections of Rowans, and have our very own Alice Starmore discontinued shade card to boot. Picasso's sketchbooks turning up on eBay would not have caused a greater frenzy. Even for us, despite our skewed financial orientation (the eBay yarn budget took priority over the light bill), it was a stretch to think that we had to possess these books. And that we would throw in together to buy this huge, pricey pile of possibly moldy old stuff that might smell bad—well. It was a pinky promise and a stick-a-needle-in-your-eye commitment.

I watched the final moments of the auction tick away, waiting for eSnipe to make our sneak-attack bid, and we won. The phone rang. Yikes! I just about jumped out of my skin. It was like Ed McMahon calling to say I'd won the Publishers Clearing House sweepstakes. "Rilly? It's *you*?" I said, stupid. What's funny is that I had had the same impulse to call her to mark this ridiculous moment. She was glad I didn't sound like a character on *The Dukes of Hazzard*. I was relieved that she didn't say "Okeydokey." We hung up, then headed off to fork over the PayPal payment of the year. In a couple of weeks, fifty pounds of old Rowan magazines and the rare, discontinued treasure *Knitted Clowns* landed at my house. It was a stunning coup, though we should have paid attention when it took a month for us to get around to dividing them. Procrastination is a shared trait.

One day, in an email titled "Re: Please send me total amount for item #2348672727," which had begun as an eBay-related message but veered into the discussion of why margaritas are a hazard, Kay wrote, "I must ask the burning question: Are you really Ann Patchett (which I've been telling everybody you probably are)?" I had to laugh. It turned out that Kay had been reading Nashville's Most Esteemed Author's *Bel Canto*, and remembered the *New York* magazine article that mentioned that she lived in Nashville. And in a moment of mild paranoia about the Internet, she figured: "I mean, if Ann Patchett wanted to hang out on knitting blogs, she wouldn't want everybody to know she was Ann Patchett, right? 'Cause they'd bug her, right? So she'd change her name to Ann Shayne. Obviously that's what she'd do."

We started a blog, Mason-Dixon Knitting. We figured that if we were going to write incessant emails, we might as well take it on the road. Reduce/reuse/recycle! We liked the odd world of online knitting, and we hoped people would stop by. Once we got over the crippling self-consciousness of writing for an audience of . . . nobody . . . we discovered that people would indeed jump right in, whether Kay was revealing the worst sweater she'd ever made or I explained how a book review of the new Alexander Hamilton biography left me sobbing like a widow at Bunker Hill.

Mason-Dixon Knitting ended up being like a really needy pet—who's feeding the blog today? Did anybody check on the blog? It has been a mind-blowing experience, as anyone who keeps a knitting blog will tell you. Dreadful haikus have been written, blurry photographs immortalized, and the comments of our readers never ceased to surprise us. A reader in Pennsylvania sent us a photograph she took of the Mason-Dixon

Line. Polly sent a Christmas pudding, all the way from London. Most humbling has been our charity knitting project, the Afghanalong, where people sent us eight-inch squares to be sewn up into afghans that would then go to the needy in Afghanistan. You'd have to have a heart of stone not to be moved by the care and skill shown in those squares.

Kay and I have written thousands of emails and hundreds of entries for Mason-Dixon Knitting, and we have found that we can blow a lot of time on the phone. We wrote a book proposal, sold it to a publisher, and began work on the book. In a life that sometimes seemed all too set on its course, my friendship with Kay has provided that thing that seems hard to find: never-ending pure freakin' surprise.

This party I'm looking for, for example. It's all larded up with surprise. Our hostess, Phyllis, is someone Kay met online. The women coming to help sew up afghans are people I know only by email, if at all. But several of them have blogs, so I have definite ideas about what they might be like. Even Polly from London is planning to attend; she's come home to New York for her sister's wedding. And the squares—Kay has been posting photos of all the squares people have sent for the Afghanalong, but I haven't yet seen them in their insane, varied splendor.

Kay answers the phone, tells me I'm four houses away. I'm wishing I'd worn my pointy-toed shoes but hope nobody will think I'm some pathetic clog wearer from Nashville. I still wish I'd worn a handknit, but figure that a white T-shirt and khakis will have to do. It's what I wear in just about every photo of me that I can bear to post on the blog. The first picture Kay sent me shows her in party garb, arms outstretched to display the endless moss-stitch shawl she knitted. She finished the fringe on the way to that wedding, but by golly she finished it.

As I climb the steps, the iron door swings open, and there she is, arms outstretched the same way.

"You really aren't Ann Patchett," she says, deflated.

PART THREE

What's in the Basket

There Is Something Special About: Socks

Washing My Husband's Kilt Hose: A 32-Bar Reel

Susan Blackwell Ramsey

You wash wool with shampoo. If you learn nothing
else today, learn that: to use shampoo
and water the temperature of a baby's bath.
What I have in the sink here aren't argyles,

but proper kilt hose I knit stitch by stitch, gray
for daytime, formal whites, choosing among
dozens of possible cuffs, customized gussets
to accommodate the bulging calves

of Scottish country dancers, whose heels must never
touch the floor, perpetual Barbie-feet

moving through jigs, reels, strathspeys, till sweat
    and effort
equal ease and grace. The ones who say

"the important thing is just to have fun" miss
the most fun and the point, which is not fun
but joy, daughter of the difficult.
It's the kind of lesson climate teaches,

climates where sheer survival is success,
complaint as bad as cowardice, the humor deadpan,
self-control a given, not a goal—
an attitude empires find useful. Thermopolae, Dunkirk;

to delay catastrophe they place the best
regiments behind, the Spartans, Scots,
murdered or interned for the duration.
The Spartans combed and died. The Scots composed

a dance for captured warriors, "The Reel
of the 51st." Bemused Nazi guards
watched them practice, muscles taut as barbed wire.
It's hell to dance. These socks are stomped to felt,

dancing defiance of captors long since dead. No one
would knit these hose for any amount of money
a Scot would pay. Only one currency
is deep enough. I pat them out to dry.

Have a Mice Weekend

Kay Flores

Socks grow a personality depending on where they're knitted. I've knitted energetic red and orange socks during a wild Wyoming wind, adventurous blue and green socks while floating past glaciers and killer whales, and serene, earth-tone socks at church camp. I knitted hiking socks at Ann's cabin in the Bighorn Mountains of Wyoming and those socks . . . well, they're unique.

The view from the cabin is as spectacular as the wildlife. From the porch, you can see the Cloud Peak Glacier, elevation 13,175 feet. We've watched spruce grouse, mountain bluebirds, deer, antelope, and moose near the cabin, and seen brook trout dancing on their tails in the creek. The cabin wasn't a palace when it was built in the late 1800s, and it's still not. It features a wood-burning stove, and we carry water from nearby Clear Creek. There's a rustic privy out back and an occasional rodent in the cabin. Ann and I both love the mountains, knitting, and talking, but we don't like rodents.

We headed for the cabin one summer evening. After a late dinner, we settled in to knit. Before long, I found my hiking sock yarn was in the kind of huge snarl that takes four hands to unsnarl. An hour later, we decided it would take four hands AND daylight. Time for bed.

I unfolded the sleeper sofa where I sleep. I sighed deeply

when I saw the mouse nest on the mattress. I don't like mouse nests because they remind me of mice, but I grabbed a plastic bag to dispose of the fuzz. In retrospect, it seems obvious. What was I expecting—Easter eggs?

"EEEEK!" The sight of those four baby mice made me shriek. (Some friends don't believe this part of the story. They say I am too calm to shriek. They would know better if they had been in my house the night a visiting pet rat got loose, or the time I found the mouse in the bag of dog food. I can shriek.)

I decided the best way to handle a nest of mice was to ignore it. I started to fold the sleeper sofa back, just as the little mice began crawling out of the nest. I breathed deeply, and before hyperventilation hit, I moved the baby mice outside the cabin to fend for themselves, carefully sweeping them into a dustpan. The whole process was hampered by my certain belief mama mouse would attack me when she discovered the empty nest. Maybe mama mice don't attack outside of Wyoming. Actually, I've never seen one attack in Wyoming, but I once saw a mama jackrabbit chase my dad onto the car hood because he picked up her baby. Picture a mama bear whose cub is threatened. Picture how you would react if someone threw your babies out to fend for themselves. I'm sure mama mice attack.

Ann informed me she couldn't help me with the baby mice, but she did hold the light and later she knitted with me when I couldn't sleep. We knitted until our eyes wouldn't stay open. The minute our eyes drooped shut, the mouse party began. Those rodents ran in herds, going strong in spite of the whole box of mouse poison they'd eaten. Hours later, after two minutes of sleep, we got up to do the cabin chores: hauled wood, fixed the fence, and carried water. I worked on the hiking socks while Ann caught two big brook trout. You can't compare a big brookie to say, a salmon, but they were big as brookies go.

Later, we hiked to the neighbors' cabin, where Ann shared tales of how last fall's packrat ran brazenly across occupied furniture and thumbed its nose while eating instant-kill rat poison. Eventually it had to be shot to get it out of the cabin.

Back at the cabin, I read aloud from *KnitLit (too)* while Ann cooked the brookies for dinner. We cleaned up and settled in for more knitting and chatting. In the middle of a sentence, Ann went silent. I looked up, expecting to see her in a dropped stitch crisis. Instead, her huge eyes were staring at a point just behind me.

"Ann?"

"Oh, Jesus," she prayerfully breathed.

My mind was racing. Grizzly? Maybe, but probably not in the Bighorns. Bigfoot? I should have bought film. Serial killer? It's too bad I was using size five Brittany double points. Note to self: future cabin knitting projects (if I live that long) should be planned with self-defense in mind.

"ANN! WHAT?!"

"Packrat!" she gasped. I remembered last year's packrat.

"Where?"

"I can't see it now."

I was perched cross-legged on the couch. "Is it safe to put my feet on the floor?" She nodded, and I scurried across to her couch.

Knitting away, we watched. The packrat popped out from the woodpile. I stamped my foot. It retreated. We knitted. The packrat appeared. I stamped. It disappeared. After several rounds of this game, I admitted, "I can't sleep here with a packrat." We tried the car, but there was an impossible lump where the seat doesn't fold flat.

Resigned, we went back inside and knitted some more. When the packrat popped out again, Ann said, "I'll pay for a room in Buffalo if we can get a smoking room." Smoking isn't good for us, but who am I to argue with a great plan? In a rodent-inspired frenzy, we threw first our knitting and then the rest of our gear into the car and headed off to Buffalo. Although 11:00 P.M. is not a good time to find a room during tourist season, we persevered. The last room in town wasn't cheap, but it was pest-free, if a bit smoky.

The next morning, we bought lots more rodent poison on our way to St. Christopher's in the Bighorns. At the chapel, I prayed for respite from rodents and for forgiveness for the poison and for understanding of why God put rodents on the earth in the first place.

We felt tougher in the daylight—after all, packrats are nocturnal. Just to be safe, I stamped my feet to announce our presence as we entered. The packrat brazenly greeted us, popping out from behind the curtains.

I finished the hiking socks in the relative calm of home. They're great hiking socks, forest green and woolly. They have the brazen personality of a packrat, and my son loves them.

Ann and I have to go back to the cabin soon. I'll pack a sock project, but I'm going to sleep in my tent.

Socks in the City

Lilly Allison

If there's a way to go overboard on a project, I'll find it. I'm not content with the status quo; I am compelled to go the extra mile. I vividly remember a knitted scarf project in 4-H that ended up long enough to wrap around several people's necks at the same time. I don't know why I didn't stop at a reasonable length; I just wanted it to be longer than everyone else's. To make matters worse, I was learning as I went, and so about three feet into the scarf a rib pattern began to emerge (and I use the word "pattern" loosely, as it was hit and miss). As I got better, I began to knit more loosely, which made it expand width-wise. It was quite a sight. I don't remember anyone actually wearing it, but it did stimulate a lot of conversation.

Years later, with that behind me, I got the urge to knit again. It happened when I saw a really cute hat that looked easy (looks can be deceiving, as it had that elusive rib pattern in it). My daughter was in college in Arkansas and acquiring a winter wardrobe. This would be a perfect accessory. It looked trendy and warm. It took me quite a while to remember how to knit and how to purl, then still longer to remember that the wicked knit/purl pattern had to line up to make the rib obvious. It took weeks to make that little eight-inch hat, but finally, I finished. I realized it would be easier if I used spacers and counted every stitch, which did help when I made the next one for her roommate, then one for a local friend of hers (and her little sister) and one for a friend at church. I was on a roll.

I decided to move on to something more challenging and made a quick and easy blanket for my daughter. I felt guilty for not making anything for my son so I made another quick and easy blanket for him, all this during the summer. I thought maybe I could turn this into a new fad diet program—roast those pounds off knitting under a blanket during a hot Dallas summer. I knitted every chance I got; during movies, choir practice, road trips, and doctors' visits. (I refrained from knitting during church, although I did knit before and after.) I was slightly obsessed.

But it wasn't enough. Nothing was unique. After all, everyone made hats and blankets. A friend of mine raised sheep and I wondered if I could make my own wool yarn, which would be different. Then I thought of all the things I could make if I had all the wool from my own sheep. My husband quickly nixed that idea, reminding me sheep weren't allowed in the city limits. I abandoned that idea and resorted to perusing craft books for ideas.

Socks! It would be really cool to tell my friends I was making socks. I didn't know anyone else who made their own socks.

So in my quest to go above and beyond, I got all the supplies to make socks: more needles, a large safety pin, and more yarn. I thought it was really nice that the needles came in a four-pack. They looked like they could be easily lost since they were shorter and didn't have a stopper at one end. Imagine my surprise when I found out I had to use all four needles at the same time, and not stab myself in the process. I learned more from making that one sock than I had in making the previous five hats, two blankets, and one funky scarf (mainly because those were all basically the same pattern, just different colors and sizes). This really was a challenge.

It took forever to make that sock. I ripped out so many rows so many times that that yarn was fraying. But I persevered. Eventually I held a little sock in my hand. I had made a sock! I was so excited. My excitement quickly diminished when it dawned on me that I needed two socks to complete that "pair of socks" concept. I had to make another one. The second sock was mercifully easier than the first one, which is probably why it turned out so much larger than the first. Yes indeed. I had a very large sock and a very small sock. Hmm. If I made another sock, would it match up with one of the odd-sized socks or would I have to keep making socks till I got a match?

On second thought, I just saw a cute sweater in a magazine. How can you mess up a sweater?

Socks and Society

Betty Jones

I wonder if anybody has ever done a study about the influence of recreational activities on footwear choices. I'm not just talking about fiber arts here. Soccer players often wear those nubbly-bottom sandals even when they haven't just finished a game. Outdoor types wear their hiking boots to the grocery store. And handspinners—well, we wear anything that will show off our socks.

I think at first it's a practical thing. When you first start spinning on a wheel, it's easier to get the knack of it without shoes on. So those first few guild meetings, you wear something you can slip off of your feet easily. Then you start noticing the feet around you. You're thinking, "Wow, look at those socks. And look how great they look when she puts on those shoes!" But you don't necessarily change anything yet.

Then, on your next shopping trip, you end up quite by accident at the display that sells all the funky clogs and sandals. You have to buy a new pair because you need them—I mean, it's just too hard to untie those tennis shoes all the time. You start wearing them to meetings, and sometimes other places. You spin enough yarn and knit that first pair of socks, and then you have to wear your new shoes to show off those socks. More socks follow; you have fewer occasions to wear shoes that tie, and soon your tennis shoes are languishing on the floor of the closet.

The footwear thing is more than a symptom, though. I think it actually has an effect on personality. It may be because you are perceived to be a certain type of person if you wear wild socks and Birkenstocks, so you decide that you really are what you seem to be. At forty-something, I love to be seen as eccentric and artistic, unaffected by the opinions of others and willing to make my own fashion choices. Is that really who I am? I'm not sure, but I do know that ten years ago that side of me was still dormant. This craft, and the people involved in it, have changed me forever, and for the better. As an added bonus, I have a spectacular wardrobe of socks—and extremely comfortable feet!

A Year Knit in Socks

Susan West Kurz

I went to a sock knitting class last spring. I remember a lot about the actual day because I had a severe case of poison ivy that I'd caught the week before, trying to save an old cedar from the clutches of the woody vines that entwined it from roots to tip. After a week of failed attempts at natural cures, I called my doctor just after sunrise, insane from lack of sleep and itchy blisters. I had just enough time to pick up a prescription of steroids, swallow them with orange juice, glide over the Coolidge Bridge, and arrive early enough to choose yarn and needles before the class began at 10:00.

Fantasies of socks in every color for everyone I knew, for any occasion, danced through my head. Cashmere for my son who lives in L.A., lightweight cotton adorned with flamingos for my sister in Florida, sensible wool for my mother who is threatening to die again this year before her birthday, maybe Italian worsted lichen green for me. Gifts, centering, enjoyment, all rolled neatly into a ball of any color. I had signed up to join the time-tested sisterhood of knitters. The women I knew knit at school functions, in board meetings, during lectures, on planes, caught in traffic, in waiting rooms, and at the beach. I would become one of them.

I decided on socks for my newly adopted Guatemalan children, Emilio and Rossibel. That made the color choice easy: two skeins of multicolored yarn that waved to me like a flag from Central America—bold orange, red and gold, blue, green, and purple. The children would love wearing them on their dancing feet.

The class was using a sock pattern hot off the Web, designed for circular needles. A little clumsy at first, the teacher warned, but then so easy, so satisfying. The ten of us sat around a table made for six, piled high with books and magazines displaying a multitude of designs. Linda, our teacher, danced her own project along as she helped us cast on and start knitting. At first, conversation was limited to "oohs" and "ahs" and "please help me, I'm all mixed up." By 11:00 one confident student, new to socks but not to sweaters, was inches ahead of the class. She offered to run across the street to Gwen's Deli to get coffee for all of us.

I knew I was in the right place. As we grew more confident, the click of needles mingled with quiet conversations. The bell on the door jingled as another knitter dropped in to pick up supplies. Linda read through the directions, warning us that the knitting would get tricky when we made the transition from the sock leg to the heel. She invited us to come back for help anytime we needed it. My breathing slowed as the sock top grew from my needles. As I had hoped, all thoughts of poison ivy vanished.

After that morning, the socks progressed slowly. Knitting on airplanes was no longer possible. On land, I carried my supplies in a cloth shoebag over my shoulder, hoping to steal time for a few rows now and then. By summer, I was ready to start the heel but I couldn't remember what Linda had said back in April about the tricky part.

The heel was indeed tricky, and on my travels I found that not all yarn shop owners knew how to knit a sock with circular needles. I scrambled to find time to visit Northampton Wools between business meetings and occupational therapy appointments for Rossibel, waiting for the chance to ask Linda for instruction. She guided me successfully from heel to toe. By Halloween, I was finished with the first sock and confident that the second would be finished for Rossibel when I returned from a business trip to Europe. So much time had lapsed since my first heel transition that I got stuck in the same spot on the second sock, but this time in Sienna. The ladies in the shop that sold knitting supplies, beeswax candles, and handmade paper journals apparently had never knit socks on circular needles either. They looked at each other and laughed. I heard the word "American" as I left their shop.

I finished my first pair the Saturday before Thanksgiving. The day was bittersweet. Rossibel was delighted, and my family indulged my pride over my success. But later in the day, our fourteen-year-old cat Lucy died. We lit a candle and read a cat poem by Rumer Godden as we buried Lucy in the woods. We went inside drying our eyes, and built a fire, and I cast on 44 stitches for Emilio's first sock.

Snow and sorrow arrived early. A close friend simultaneously confronted breast cancer and the suicide of her husband. I walked beside my friend as she bore her loss and met the challenges of her cancer. I grabbed moments before the fire, sliding my needles around, under, and through the bright yarn. There were times during those days when I didn't know what to do but knit. Simply to knit a child's sock became an oasis for me. Each time I picked up my socks, I felt the support of women knitting, thousands and thousands of them over hundreds of years.

Rossibel lost her socks then found them again. My friend came through her surgery and chemotherapy. My son arrived late on Christmas Eve from California, slept through Christmas, woke up after New Year's, and left. Emilio's first sock ended with donkey ears as I finished the toe a little too quickly. I began my fourth sock determined to finish by Easter.

I moved from the heel to the instep of my fourth sock on a late-March Saturday night, almost a year after that first class with Linda. The next morning I opened the shades to a sunny morning; white birches stood out against the naked oaks and evergreens in the east meadow. I made a pot of Irish Breakfast tea and went back to bed, with the well-worn sock pattern lying on my quilt. I reread the directions out loud and once again counted the multicolored stitches on my circular needles. I took off my glasses, leaned back, sipped the warm sweet tea, and yelled, "I think I got it right!"

As Linda said, "Follow the directions. Look at the sock; does it make sense? It doesn't have to be perfect but always count the stitches—that's important." I still gasp when I drop a stitch, but I've learned to pick it up and just keep going. I have come to love these handmade socks with their beautiful imperfections.

I've planned a family reunion for October to celebrate my mother's ninetieth birthday. It will be the first time in her life that her four children, their spouses, her ten grandchildren and her eight great-grandchildren could all be together. I've decided on pale blue-gray merino wool to get her through another New England winter.

Stop Looking at My Booty (or, Cautionary Tales from the Post-modern Knitting Circle at the Mel-O-Dee)

Cheryl Mandala

My friends and I have a booty problem. Baby booties, that is. It started out as a quick and fun project. We're at that age where suddenly everyone you know is pregnant. I mean everyone—Your neighbor. Your coworker. That woman you always see at the coffee shop on Webster. Your best friend. Everyone.

After dealing with the initial wave of shock and alarmed introspection (how did we all get to be thirty? When did my friends become so grown up when it's all I can do to match my socks in the morning? If you're having a baby, does that mean we're going to stop going to bars?) there's this secondary wave of excitement. Because where there are babies there is knitting for babies. It's perfect, really. First of all, babies (and hence, baby clothes) are so little that you can embark on great experiments with a definite end in sight. Plus there are so many great little knitted things that you couldn't convince a sentient being to wear, but which parents will gladly stuff their babies into.

But back to our booty problem. It began with a single booty. In red, which says, "I have a baby, but I'm still hip and edgy." And with a little red ribbon, which says "I may be hip and edgy, but my baby is still cuter than your baby." It was, as my mother would say, darling. It was adorably cute. So cute that you wish that you too could wear booties. Like, to work. So at that point you were feeling pretty proud of yourself.

But every booty needs a twin, naturally. You can't just rest on the laurels of a single booty. So you return to your pattern, your yarn, and your favorite chair. And along came booty number two—the first booty's twin.

But they weren't twins. Not even close. Except in a Danny DeVito and Arnold Schwarzenegger kind of way. Because booty number two was . . . huge. Gargantuan. Comically, bizarrely, inexplicably huge. But how? You used the same pattern, the same yarn. And for the love of God—you knit them over the same weekend. How could things have gone so terribly wrong? When did baby booty number two develop a mind of its own?

Thus began an odyssey of sorts. An obsessive booty-making

frenzy. Books were consulted. Baby feet were measured. We started a booty-a-thon, determined to solve the mystery of booty number two. We made booties from all kinds of yarn and all kinds of patterns.

But the booty-a-thon only deepened the mystery, because now we have this whole collection of misshapen booties. Thimble-sized booties. Booties almost as big as your head. Strange, boxy, malproportioned booties.

We've begun naming them, and trying to find alternate uses for them. Several could pass for booties if felted. Most clearly could not. One is perhaps a holder for (very small) sewing notions. Curiously, one is the perfect size and shape for a hitchhiker's mitten.

Eventually we called off the booty-a-thon. I'm trying not to get too worked up about the whole thing. You might say that I've given up on my quest for the perfect booty. Which maybe means I'm growing up after all.

In the wake of my booty disasters I've turned my attention to little baby hats and little baby sweaters. They're coming along nicely. Except for the one that morphed into some kind of bizarre alpaca sportsbra. Which is an entirely different story.

Francesca

Maggie Calvin

The new sock settles itself down on my needles—I'm of the two-circular-needles persuasion, don't shoot me! I'm working with my favorite sock yarn, a sturdy Norwegian wool-and-nylon blend, a weight perfect for hiking socks. It makes socks ideal for toasting your toes by a wood fire on a Sunday afternoon in a Maine January. Toe-toasting is more my speed than hiking, especially at this time of year.

On the sofa next to my knitting chair sits my knitting daughter Francesca, who has finished the two-by-two ribbing of her first sock and is heading down the leg. She's working in a bright self-patterning yarn on size 2 Turbo steel needles, on loan from my circular needle stash. She swore she'd never knit socks. She swore she'd never knit on skinny little needles. Now she's hooked.

What is it about socks? I never thought about handknit socks until my mother-in-law made me a pair. I was almost afraid to wear them, they were so beautiful. I did my own first pair on size 6 double-pointed needles, awkwardly juggling the fragile frame from which the new fabric dangled. I read the directions for turning the heel and couldn't follow them at all; they made no sense. A sock-expert knitting friend showed me, and that was that. I was in love. There was magic in the back-and-forth, the short rows piling up to cup the heel; I was fascinated by the formation of the gusset and the smooth flow of decreases down to the foot. Those first socks (red acrylic, lousy yarn) were no hell, but the next pair went better.

Now I don't need to look at the pattern anymore. I just knit, for friends, for family, for the church bazaar: plain socks, cabled socks, self-patterning socks, socks with bands of lace, socks ribbed or not ribbed all the way to the toe. I haven't tried intarsia socks or argyle socks, but those are no doubt in the wings. While other knitters lavish money on fabulous yarns, I build my stash of fast slim circular Turbos so that I can have a sock project in each room of the house. I have abandoned sweaters and turned my back on vests; I have reneged on afghans and foresworn baby blankets. I do have a muffler on the go, and that's about it. Having several socks on the stocks means that there's always one in the idiot straight knitting phase (leg or foot) and one in the introverted complicated phase (heel or toe), so that I can knit without thinking or vanish into the zen of shaping. And socks are small. I can stuff a sock in my purse and surreptitiously work on it at an office meeting, holding it under the table, putting it down to make the occasional note.

Francesca (who is strong-minded) was absolutely anti-sock until we got to be a knitting mother/daughter act. She's a college student, second year, new to my church; she's far from home, and we brought her to our house and fed her chicken with dumplings and lasagna and all the comfort foods she missed. She babysits my young 'uns. She is teaching me Italian cooking and my husband is teaching her plumbing. She's a pre-med student; she thinks she'll find plumbing useful. She learned to knit from her Italian grandmother, and she is determined and intelligent. She has plowed away at a complicated Aran, frogging ruthlessly.

But she's apt to make blanket (afghan?) knitting decisions which, I think, sometimes need to be challenged. She says firmly that life is too short for fair isle or intarsia. For the longest time, she refused to consider knitting flat stuff on circular needles, until I handed her the muffler and got her to try, after which she was as absolutely converted. And she was utterly opposed to socks; no way was she going there. Where this resistance came from, I never found out, except that Francesca is in general a person of extremely strong opinions—you should hear her on Cecilia Bartolli. But I bided my time; I took her to our local yarn shop, where we drifted about for a blissful hour. I showed her the sample sock in self-patterning yarn, let her caress the ball with her long, white, tapering fingers—her hands belong in a Renaissance portrait. The yarn caught her. She turned away from her anti-sock position with a thunderous flash, tossing back her long black hair; she was seduced, and succumbed.

Now she knits at her sock with a passion that sometimes topples over into obsession. That's how I know Francesca is a real knitter, like her Nana. She knits with ferocity, strong convictions, and utter concentration, and she is a perfectionist. The pattern emerging from the yarn entrances her; she crows when a length of bright yellow springs from the bowels of the ball. My five-year-old crawls up beside her and Francesca puts an arm around the girl and cuddles her—and goes on knitting.

I cannot wait for the magical moment when I teach her how to turn a heel.

My Godfather's Socks

Susanna Heath

I rent silly movies while I knit my godfather's socks.

I rent Indiana Jones movies; I rent *Men in Black;* I rent *Beetlejuice*; I rent *Ghostbusters*, both one and two. I watch *Men with Brooms* for what must be the ninth or tenth time, still giggling over all the Canadian in-jokes. I rent anything that will amuse me without calling on any particular attention. I just need the entertainment while I knit my godfather's socks.

I like socks, but this is a fine yarn, 9 stitches to the inch on skinny needles, and his feet (I asked, without letting him know why) are a 10 EEE. There are 88 stitches in each round. This sock will require the Lord alone knows how many hundreds, even thousands, of stitches—just plain knitting round and round on two circular needles (my preferred sock-knitting method) before I got to the exciting bit, the heel flap, the heel turn, the gusset—and then many hundreds (maybe thousands) of tiny knit stitches before the toe. That would be only one sock. I have to do two. And I want to get them done for Christmas.

He isn't really my godfather. I was baptized, with godparents who were never really part of my life, when I was tiny. He came into my life when I was six and he was twenty-one, and he drifted into and out of my home for years thereafter. He passed for a friend of my parents', and in his own way I do believe he loved them, but he looked at the way they operated—the simmering tensions, the drink, the sniping, the underlying rage, the infidelities—and he held himself a little away from them. Last summer, when I visited him, he told me that when he came back to our house, it was only a little bit to see my parents. Mostly he came to see us, my brothers and sisters. And me. He came to see me, he said. I didn't know that. It was a gift of enormous proportions.

I remember him as a benign and interested party. I remember him walking into our kitchen when I was sixteen and a hopeless wallflower with no belief that any person of the male persuasion would ever deign to look at me, and he said, "How's your love life, kid?" and I burst into tears, and he hugged me, sat me down at the kitchen table, listened to me, and consoled me. He heard me, as no one else in my life did. It made a difference.

I can talk to him about the past, because he remembers. He has told me stories about my parents that both enrich and darken my understanding of them, stories that make them more human, but also more shadowed and imperfect. But that diminishes the power they had over me, and for that I am grateful.

He makes me remember to give thanks for all the other-relationships in my life: for his other-parenting, for my other-children, for my other-sisters and other-brothers, for all who have stood in the place of family to me. And I am grateful for all those who have allowed me to be other-parent or -child or -sister to them. As my godfather reminds me, family isn't always where you can turn to for support, because sometimes they just can't, or don't, or won't, and it's stupid to beat your heart to rags against a rock. But you can choose family, if you want, and other-family can be inestimably precious.

My godfather is a sturdy man with a broad Irish nose, a priest who practices Zen, who is placid and calm and accepting of who I am. He gave me the cross he used to use when preaching, a huge, strong silver thing, full of stories: David and his harp, Paul greeting Timothy, Jacob wresting with the angel at the river's bank. I clutch it when I'm in trouble, and my trouble flows off into the heavy silver, into my godfather's keeping.

The sock I am knitting for him droops from my needles, growing slowly. I am making it in one of those self-patterning yarns; it forms itself into stripes and almost-Argyle patterns in lively shades. I will tell him to wear these socks when he's Zen-meditating; I will remind him, when he wears them, to remind himself that he was a powerful force for good in my life. I know that's trite. So's knitting socks. I don't care.

These socks will be done in time to send them for Christmas. No other projects matter this much. Everything else can wait.

Some Work, Some Don't: Projects

Aran Go Blah!

Penelope Allen

Sliding down ladders of dropped stitches.
A knitter's lament, my sleepless song.
I'm caught on broom lace rungs knit by witches.

My muscles are plagued with twitches.
Sheepless woolly hooves clattering along
sliding down ladders of dropped stitches.

Popcorn bobbles in a collection of glitches.
How come that panel went so wrong?
I'm caught on broom lace rungs knit by witches.

Cables snake past their purled ditches
into a moss stitch billabong
sliding down ladders of dropped stitches.

The casting off heaves and it pitches
while the clock chimes another ding-dong.
I'm caught on broom lace rungs knit by witches.

There's no R&R from these hitches.
This night is going to be far too long.
Sliding down ladders of dropped stitches
I'm caught on broom lace rungs knit by witches.

The Seven-Pound Fleece

Dianne Little

I am a knitter. Have been since I was sixteen and knitted my first pair of mittens on four needles. I am also a spinner. Have been since 1970. The problem arose when my two fiber avocations collided. Have you ever tried to knit with your own handspun?

I wanted to make a beautiful cape out of handspun. This cape was to be one of my first handspun hand-knit projects. I found a seven-pound gray marbleized fleece that would work perfectly and look great. Now, this weight is important to the story, so remember the number. I brought the dirty, smelly fleece home and went through all the preparation—sorting, washing, flick-combing the locks. I spun a worsted weight yarn. I didn't wash or block the yarn until I had completed spinning all the wool. Took some time, didn't it?

The first problem arose when I washed all that two-ply

yarn. Instead of the knitting worsted I'd spun, the yarn quickly "bloomed" (as we spinners like to call it) into a very bulky weight. No problem! I know about gauge. I'll just reconnoiter—knit a swatch, figure out the math, and make it work. So the cape will be a little thicker than what I envisioned. After all, I live in Michigan where it can get cold. I could now wear it in the dead of winter in Michigan. Right?

After reconnoitering, I started to knit. This cape pattern started at the bottom. You decreased as you knit up the cape. I had all those little blue, yellow, and white markers telling me "decrease here." Of course, when you have a billion stitches scrunched up on a circular needle, you cannot see how large or small the actual garment will be. I was a little concerned when it took a whole skein of yarn to knit one row. What did I know? It would be all right. After all, when you keep decreasing it will get smaller and use up less yarn. Right?

After a few nights of knitting, (I actually had a real job during the day) I became slightly concerned about whether I would have enough yarn to complete the project. When you knit with handspun there is no nice pattern to tell you to buy fifteen 50-g skeins of the designated yarn. I could only hope and pray that I would have enough yarn because I couldn't just go out and buy some more yarn. Forget about the dye lot.

At midnight, nine inches of straight (not circular) knitting later, I decided that I *really* needed to take a look. I was close to gauge, or as close as I thought handspun could get. I took a tapestry needle and some yarn, threaded the yarn through all the stitches and markers (making it easier to replace them on the knitting needle later), and removed the stitches so that I could see the garment up close and personal.

My living room is twenty-one feet long. When I removed

the stitches and laid the unfinished knitting on the floor, there was one foot left between the wall and the end of the cape. What happened? I know I did the math correctly. After all, I am a math teacher. I curled the twenty-foot length of cape-to-be into a circle just as if I was going to wear it as a cape and I laughed until the tears ran down my face. Good thing my husband was sound asleep so he couldn't see the spectacle I was making of myself.

OK, let's start over. After all, I have the patience of Job. Reconnoiter, figure the math, put on the stitches again, and knit. Everything looked just fine and it took a lot less yarn than the first attempt. Many hours and then days and months passed and the cape was finally completed. I was so thrilled. You knitters know the feeling when that last stitch is cast off. Trying on the cape was such a gratifying experience. It was the correct length; it fit me at the shoulders, not too big, and not too small. Fantastic!

Then I went to put my hands and arms through the arm slits. Oh, no! There was one problem left. The cape fit, the arm slits came out at the bust line. Picture me trying to shake hands with someone. Somehow, the rows-per-inch gauge didn't work.

Oh—one more thing. Remember the seven pounds? This cape somehow gained weight when it was knitted. It now weighed twenty-five pounds. How could that happen? The seven pounds was an unwashed fleece with all that lanolin and vegetable matter!

I took it all apart again, reskeined the wool, and washed it. It is still waiting to be something.

The moral to this story is "Listen to your yarn. It will tell you what it wants to be." My yarn did not want to be a cape. It really wanted to be a rug.

A Winning Sweater

Lorraine Lener Ciancio

The young cottonwood has already shed its yellow leaves. It is early September 2004 and autumn has been in the air for two weeks. While numerous hurricanes are striking Florida in rapid succession, here in the mountains of northern New Mexico the days are green and yellow under tranquil blue skies. Nights are cold. The blanket I knitted in June won a blue ribbon at the county fair last month. When I wrap myself in it images of cotton candy, baby pigs, and monstrous zucchinis erupt.

Is it possible that the things I've created retain an afterimage that gets embedded in them through long days of concentration and exposure? When I pick up that striped sweater I always see Rick and Ilsa saying goodbye in the foggy airport. The yellow socks evoke a sad day in another September; they speak of shattered illusions and vulnerability. The thick socks I finished this morning were made from smoky blue handspun bought from a friend. She is selling her possessions to buy a ticket to Nepal where she will become a Buddhist nun. I will think of her every time I wear those socks.

Then there is the purple cardigan. That's what I want to tell you about.

One gray day in late October, almost four years ago, I decided to start a project that would simultaneously pull me into and through the season of declining light. I chose a wool and silk yarn of deep purple tweed and a pattern for an Aran cardigan with a pretty border and flattering collar. The design was a complicated leaf diamond cable. Panels of moss stitch separated the cables while a wavy hem and twisted stitches created a sharp corded effect. The pattern was daunting. I had never attempted anything as ambitious. I began with the narrow front panel. The welt border was beautiful. We were just a few days away from the presidential election and I knew that my husband, a political junkie, would watch the results for hours as they came in on election night. I planned to sit in the next room, half listening, knitting.

Between my buying the yarn and election day, my son called to tell us that he was going to be arrested. We had recently learned of his addiction to prescription drugs. He had hired the best defense lawyer in the state but would most likely still go to prison. Inwardly I protested. We didn't descend from a line of drug addicts, abusers, felons. That happened in other families. We came from Italian immigrants who worked hard, built brick houses in suburbs, saved money, and believed in American values.

I cried, I knitted, I voted. A new president was elected. Or was he? I listened and knitted. I noticed, a few days into recounts and debates that my cables didn't look anything like the photo on the pattern. Mine were fuzzy, undefined. Where were the crisp shapes? In Florida officials were counting ballots, using silly unfamiliar names to describe them. I ripped out the almost-completed left front down to the border. My son was sick. His immune system was so depleted that he had caught a severe flu.

Halfway through the second attempt at the front panel, I realized I had been doing the twisted stitch wrong. And my diamonds still didn't look like the ones in the photo. The possibility that we might not have a president by inauguration day had cadres of historians appearing on television to tell about past elections, orders of succession laid out by our Founding Fathers, and the consequences of an undetermined election. I called the designer of the pattern. She agreed to check out the instructions because, after all, mistakes do happen. She called back next day. They were correct. I ripped out the front, including the flawless border. In Florida they were counting votes again.

My son was recovering from the flu. His lawyer wanted to meet with me. The sweater was moving along. I easily completed the simpler sleeves. I made arrangements to fly to New York. The vote count in New Mexico was so close that newspapers editorialized over an old law involving a poker game that might have to be resorted to. Nationally, there was talk of bringing in the Supreme Court to resolve the election issue. The vote count in Florida was on again and off again. Information emerged that on election day, polling places had illegally closed down early, turning away hundreds of voters; others had been deemed ineligible felons. There seemed to be an inordinate number of felons living in Florida. I didn't want to hear about felons and kept on knitting. I managed to complete the two front panels although they still didn't look like the picture.

At last I was ready for the back. The piece de resistance. Four panels of cables. I figured no one would notice the front, but the back was critical. If it didn't turn out right the whole world would see it as I stood on checkout lines wearing it.

A third of my mind was occupied with charts and stitches, a third was abashed, a third empty. Somehow this configuration yielded the knitting results I had been struggling with for weeks. I continued on, confident of at least one outcome.

The Supreme Court declared a winner; the loser conceded; historians breathed a sigh of relief; pundits continued to debate; the Constitution would not collapse. I would see my son in a few weeks. All but the collar of the sweater was finished. I had purchased four lovely pewter buttons. Then I suddenly saw the front panels for what they were and ruthlessly ripped. I noticed mistakes in the sleeves and ripped them too, with no regrets. After weeks of knitting, I had only the back of a sweater and a basket overflowing with balls of yarn.

Starting over, I finished the sweater before the trip. It fit perfectly and I could find no mistakes, except for one small hole on the side—the door through which my spirit could escape and remain free.

The next summer the purple sweater won first place at the county fair. My son served a short sentence in a minimum security prison and emerged as one of the handful of people who actually learn from the experience. I named the sweater My Master's Thesis in Survival and have never attempted another like it. To do so might invoke forces I do not wish to disturb. There is another presidential election coming up soon.

Ribbed for Her Pleasure

Norah Piehl

I swear it was a coin purse. Really I do.

I first learned how to knit at summer camp. Over the

course of two weeks, a small but determined band of preteen girls gathered on the shores of Lake Bemidji to learn from a young German woman named Greta. By day, we learned to knit and purl; by night, I practiced by flashlight, as I stubbornly sat on my bunk bed and taught my clumsy fingers to work the rough wool yarn.

I was proud of the little coin purse I had produced by the end of camp. I loved the blue color, and I was particularly pleased with the nifty I-cord closure. After camp, I was filled with big plans for other knitting projects, and I was eager to show off my work to my family and friends. After all, now I knew how to do something they didn't.

The night I got back home, I met my best friend Jenny for ice cream. I slyly pulled out my new blue coin purse to pay for my vanilla cone. Jenny noticed it immediately, but not for the reasons I had planned. She didn't say, "What a fabulous coin purse! You made it yourself?" or "Wow! That's great! Can you make me one?" or any of the million other things I had hoped for. Nope. Not even close.

"What the hell is that thing?" Jenny said. "Don't you know what it looks like?" I looked, puzzled, at my coin purse. Didn't it look like, well, a coin purse? Giggling, Jenny leaned over and whispered in my ear what she thought it was. Looking back at the knitted object, I turned bright red. Granted, it had always been a little odd in shape, and now that it held several dollars' worth of quarters it had stretched out even more. Innocent as I was, it had taken my sex-crazed best friend to point out that my new coin purse was the exact size and shape of, well, a certain male organ.

"You knitted a condom!" Jenny said loudly, as everyone at Dairy Queen turned around to stare at me. Never mind that a handknit condom would prevent neither sexually transmitted disease nor unwanted pregnancy. Never mind that it would probably chafe both parties. Never mind that I was only twelve years old and didn't even know what a real condom looked like. Jenny insisted on loudly showing me how the I-cord could make the "condom" adjustable and how easily the garter stitch would stretch to accommodate different sizes. Laughing loudly, she joked that I should make one in cotton rather than wool next time.

I hastily jammed the offending coin purse in my pocket and hid it away in my dresser when I got home. After Jenny and her dirty mind had shed a whole new light on my coin purse, I was too embarrassed even to show it to my parents. Is it any wonder that it took me almost twenty years to get up the nerve to try knitting again?

Thanks to Jenny, even now, I stick to scarves and sweaters. I stay away from purses, cozies, and any other knitting project whose function might be even slightly open to interpretation.

HWIP

Marsha Letourneau

The subject among the knitterly group was HWIP. I assumed that meant Hellish Work In Progress, and I have one. Later I learned the H stands for Hopeless, which I would prefer to believe this project is not. . . .

Some time ago a friend of ours asked me to mend a sweater for her toddler son, a sweet little guy who visited often and sometimes spent the night, and who has a special place in our hearts with our own grandchildren. The sweater is a handsome navy crew-neck pullover, machine knit, but not seamed well at the shoulder. Some of the stitches had laddered down—nothing difficult to knit up and secure at the seam.

At this time his mom had a newborn, a bit sickly. We hoped this baby would grow to be as robust as his lively big brother and would wear the sweater, too. Not long afterward, the infant was diagnosed with some bone fractures. The authorities immediately assumed that the injuries had been inflicted by his parents, and both sons were taken away from their home.

The rest of the story is one of those awful, nearly unbelievable tales of governmental good intentions and bureaucratic bungling in a rural, economically depressed area, unfortunately rife with domestic violence. Physical evidence and blood work supported an internal cause of injury, and the physicians agreed, including those who'd initially suspected abuse.

A pediatric orthopedist, who has devoted his career to and has authored medical texts on bone maladies in children, demonstrated with the x-rays how none of the fractures could have been caused externally. He even identified additional fractures, overlooked by the other physicians, that had happened during birth and had healed or were healing.

The presiding judge, hand-picked by the Department of Human Services, was one whose decisions were rarely in favor of parents. Attorneys for both sides believed this to be because he'd once returned a child to parents whose abuse later killed the child. Calling the evidence and expert testimonies "a nice theory," this judge ruled against the parents. The same judge presided over each judicial appeal the parents made, ruling the same in every one of those as well. It was a nightmare that dragged on for years.

Now it's been nearly a decade. Both boys were adopted, and the younger one's mineral deficiency resolved itself just as the specialist diagnosed it would. The parents moved away, though not far from the boys. We get news and a photo from time to time. I still have the sweater. I never finished the repair—there's certainly no pressing need to right now—but I won't part with the little thing either. Every time I see it folded at the bottom of the mending basket, I remember. Then I pray for reunion and healing in a heartbroken family.

To me this really is a Hellish Work in Progress, but I also continue to look at it as a Hopeful one.

A Hat Offering

Mindy Leary

Size 8 circular needles. Cast on 88 stitches. Knit knit, purl purl. And so it goes, round and round till the time seems right to start the decreases. Several rounds later I have a practical ribbed cap ready to go. In the mysterious way it always seems to happen, a client or two will stop by in desperate need of head cover later in the day.

Go back in time to one crisp September Alaskan morning, with frost framing the puddles of the alleyway. I found myself searching for a ramshackle, red building, with a take-out window and small, white cross on top: Anchorage's Downtown

Soup Kitchen. It's a faith-based outreach to the homeless, run by Change Point Church. Over the next few months I would hear its message.

I had spent the prior year in a surreal state of grief and sadness. My son's fiancée had been killed by a drunk driver. The fog that loss brings had not lifted. My heart ached. In his search for peace and understanding my son emailed me the following shortly after Nikki's death:

> *We as humans have the gift of free will, given to us by a God who loves us. We can take our free will and do one of two things: make decisions that love and respect others, or love ourselves and make decisions that hurt others. I'll bet the man who killed Nikki has been hurt pretty badly in his life. So he continued the cycle and hurt all of us. I would venture to hope that the hurt stops with us. In an unjust world, we can choose to let the injustice stop with us, and press on with broken hearts in hope that love is worth it.*

Someone suggested that I might find solace in reaching out to others. The Lord suggested the Downtown Soup Kitchen.

During my first few weeks at the kitchen all I could see was the poverty, addiction, and hunger clinging to each person like caked-on mud. Over the next several months, I would find that these weathered souls met the heartfelt kindnesses extended to them with appreciation, love, and (frequently toothless) grins. Though I was originally apprehensive about spending time with these people, with whom I seemed to have so little in common, I found myself serving the needs of the most vulnerable in our city with grace and humility—ultimately finding that I had ever so much in common with them all.

Eventually, I began knitting hats to distribute on my Tuesdays at the kitchen. It gets cold here; a hat offering is a practical and welcoming gesture of love. I tried to knit two or three a week. In one summer vacation stretch I was able to amass a collection of eighteen hats for the fall. It remains a joy to extend a homemade hat to a soul in need of the love and warmth it offers.

Last Tuesday was no different. I had been so busy over the course of the previous week that I had only had time to knit one hat. It was pretty—a muted speckled purple and turquoise chenille blend. After arriving at the kitchen I got distracted with peeling eggs for the sandwiches as well as other preparations. I lost sight of the soft knit hat.

It was cold; the wind was whipping in off Cook Inlet, chilling the air. At the usual time, around noon, a line of hungry souls meandered down the alleyway, waiting for a warm meal. The 350 cups of hot soup and dozens and dozens of sandwiches went quickly. Toward the end of my shift at the serving window I looked up to see a woman standing before me in the most brilliant, shimmering, purple coat I had ever seen. It was trimmed in turquoise. She had no hat.

"Hang on," I said, "I've got something you've gotta have. I just made it over the weekend."

One of the volunteers, helping with the spiritual and clothing needs of many there in the chapel area, located the errant hat and brought it to me. I handed it to the woman waiting at the window. She looked a bit confused. Tentatively she accepted it, slowly placing the hat on her head. It looked stunning. Though she didn't have a mirror, she broke out into the biggest grin ever, looking even more beautiful than before.

I gave her a steaming cup of soup and a sandwich. She set off back down the alleyway with her head held a littler higher, beaming with the love of Christ.

The Cardigan

Harry Kelley

For Claire Londagin, the Dancing Girl

When rain awakens sleeping fields
Dreaming earth her greenness yields,
And where respectful sheep have trod
Grows a luscious, living sod.

Then the sheep, who name each blade
By type and form as God has made,
For timothy baa, for clover bleat,
And eat and eat and eat and eat.

After ruminating there
The belled Ninotchka thought of Claire,
To stop from crying shook her head
Which rang her small sheep bell instead.

"Why must I wait until school ends?
Should learning separate best friends?
Why should the girl I love the most
Have to live on the other coast!"

"O Portland! Portland, point obscure!
So cruel to keep me far from her!
Are you a City? Desert? Star?
Do other sheep live where you are?

"I know that there's no other Claire
Full-hearted, funny, friendly, fair
As mine in Portland! And, yes, it's clear,
If she is there, she is not here.

"I've begged for maps, they laugh and say
'You cannot walk there in a day.'
But when I leave, they'll change their tune
I'm going to fly in a balloon!

"I just don't care what people think.
I love balloons! Especially pink!
If o'er the ocean, murky, green
I'll get a small, pink submarine?"

Sometimes life's harder than it seems
And far outstrips our wildest dreams.
"I'll figure how to see the lass!
But now I'll send a box of grass!"

Hepsiba, an older ewe,
Explained that grass would never do.
"Primates have wobbled since they stood:
They don't think grass is very good."

All the sheep knew in their guts
"If this is true, they must be nuts."

The old ewe sighed, she'd read each mind,
And merely said, "We must be kind."

The belled sheep stamped, and said, "I'm sure
That this cannot apply to her!
But even so, I'm dutiful
I'll eat grass til I'm beautiful!

"And then with others of my ilk
Whose fleeces are as soft as silk,
I'll tell the shepherd we're on strike
Until he makes what she will like!"

And all the sheep agreed as one
That this was something should be done.
And so they ate and did not cease
Until they'd all grown perfect fleece.

In the fall the shearer came
Expecting the sheep would be the same
As all sheep are most sore afeared
Of shearers. But what a mob appeared!

They couldn't wait for autumn's trim
And almost batted eyes at him,
And didn't twist, kick, writhe nor wrestle.
"They've grown this fleece for someone special!"

"Ah, yes," the shepherd said, "this fleece
They grew specific for my niece.
She brought them corn when they were lambs,
They don't forget, these ewes, these rams."

And so he thanked the shearer kind
Admiring his perceptive mind.
He took the fleeces from the barn,
And got his friend to spin the yarn.

He thought and thought but did not see
Just what this sheep fleece ought to be.
He worried so he could not sleep.
And finally he asked the sheep.

"Each color, all the lengths and types
Are for a reason. Brown's for stripes!
Alternate it with the white,
And don't forget to sleep tonight

"For in your dream, you'll see the shape,
That you're to knit, the texture, drape,
And maybe where you'll add a bit
Of rainbow color as you knit."

He dreamed each stitch! The stitches strong,
The way the notes jive in a song,
Composed a thing of beauty bred
So much of life's conceived in bed!

And with a start, he woke up quite
And saw it was the dead of night
But inspiration's grace had pricked
The shepherd now; his needles clicked.

And clicked. And clicked. One knit, one purl,
A thousand for the dancing girl!

And happiness danced in his hands
The kind an artist understands.

And when dawn danced in the dew
He showed it to each ram, each ewe
Who thought it lovely, even though
A man must knit what a sheep can grow.

And for a moment, all was still,
The dog stopped barking, and the shrill
Screech of bugs faded in the shade.
And all thought of the golden maid.

The rain, the earth, the sheep that roam
On sheep paths in the buoyant loam,
The bugs, the birds, the hens, the pup,
Said, "Beautiful. Now wrap it up!"

Between her birthday and the cheer
Called Christmas each and every year
He licked the stamps and put them on
The sweater box, and it was gone.

"Ah," he thought, "It's sad to send
A thing you've made to such a friend,
For as it goes, you realize sure,
How far away you are from her."

In the field that afternoon,
He sang a melancholy tune.
The belled sheep shook her head as though
She meant to say, "I know, I know."

Loose Balls: Stash

The Whole Nine Yards

Samantha Lynn

We've got stash, of course. What knitter doesn't? And I thought all of it was secure. Secure enough for the old cat, who was too blind to jump; secure enough for the new cat, who's just a pretty face. . . .

But the youngest cat, the cat we've had for nine months now, is one of the smart ones. She lets herself into the cupboards under the sink, she finds her toys when they fall inside things, and now she's running through the apartment making horrible choking sounds, like she's got a hairball that won't come out. And as I give chase, I catch a glimpse of the cat owner's worst nightmare.

She's swallowing a string.

"Hydrogen peroxide," the vet says, "and if that doesn't

induce vomiting within half an hour, by which time we will have closed for the night, here's the emergency vet's number . . ."

A quick trip to the corner store for hydrogen peroxide—overpriced, and so stale it only makes the cat lick her nose and resent me. I try again while I'm waiting for my ride to the emergency vet to arrive, but the extra dose just starts her breaking wind (prodigiously, but not quite the needed result). It's been nearly an hour before we can get her into the emergency vet's office. And time is not on a cat's side when there's a string attached.

The attending vet is clearly worried that this string of unknown length may already be passing beyond the cat's stomach, which could mean major surgery. Surgery we can't afford. But for now, the vet says, let's have one last try at an emetic, and after that, well, sometimes these things do make it all the way through on their own, so to speak.

And so we sit, and we wait, and we discuss the cat in the hushed tones of a sickroom, while the technicians in the back room fiddle about with the animal and stare, all of us willing the string to reappear from one end or the other, just not the expensive thing, please. I don't want to lose my cat over our financial situation. Another woman in the waiting area confides that her cat has downed a length of elastic. It's common enough, although we've always been so careful, until now.

An hour goes by.

The vet calls us back in with good news and bad news. The good news: one end of the "string" has turned up. The bad news: the eight inches the vet is now displaying for us isn't all of it, because it got stuck as they tried to pull it back out of the cat and they had to cut it off. I study the pallid bit of fuzz, trying to imagine where my cat could have found string in our house. Oh, no, it's that long-forgotten ball of lavender mohair-blend yarn that keeps getting shuffled around into odd places, because there isn't enough of it to make anything out of and anyway it doesn't knit up very well. Last seen, if I recall, in a basket on the top of a bookcase, but that's apparently not enough to deter a nimble young cat.

The cat is still not out of danger, but they send us home, minus $185, to wait and see if the remainder of the yarn may yet emerge without further intervention. Three to five days of examining the outputs in the litter box loom ahead, with the prospect of an unmeetable expense still at the end of it all. We go on a search-and-destroy mission to account for and baggie any unsecured yarn in the house for once and for all, but find only that one source; she'd somehow homed in on the one loose ball in a houseful of tidied-away stash as if she knew exactly what to look for. (She is, as I say, a genius among cats.)

And then the story gets its happy ending: when we've been home with her for half an hour or so, the cat suddenly hunches over and gives a heave or two, and out comes a lavender-mohair hairball. For once I don't mind that she's hacked up on my blankets. The beleaguered animal gives me a look, as if to say, "There, are you happy now?" and slinks off to sulk behind the refrigerator, where she's quite aware that she can't be extracted.

We examine our trophy. All told, the cat has snacked down more than nine feet of yarn. Surely this is the whole of it, for the stuff is too strong to have broken on its journey, but we keep up our litterbox vigil, until common sense tells us that a cat with a lingering intestinal issue wouldn't be careering around the house so vigorously. The regular vet is amazed when we bring our expensive length of yarn in with our bloomingly healthy cat for her annual exam two weeks later.

Cats can die from less, but ours is none the worse for the experience, if perhaps a little wiser. Now she sits while I work and watches my yarn, but no longer makes any attempt to catch it.

The Heartbreak of Mohair

Jennifer Jameson

Mohair is cruel. There are no do-overs with mohair. Category One mohair: it can't be ripped out without breaking; Category Two mohair: it rips out slowly into extreme frizz, its original texture destroyed for all eternity.

Back when I was married, I fell in love with the Perry Ellis "bubble" sweater made famous in *Vogue Knitting*—the updated, shorter version of the tunic sweater done in two strands of Classic Elite's famous mohair La Gran, one strand jewel-tone blue, the other green. To acquire the yarn, I made my first mail-order purchase. (This was before eBay.) Despite our other problems, my husband supported my growing taste for expensive yarn.

When I received the yarn, I immediately balled the two colors from the soft, disklike skeins. I read later that my technique contributed to extra twist and halo in the yarn, and that I should have pulled the two strands from separate skeins as I knitted. But it would turn out not to matter very much.

While my marriage continued its downward spiral, I knitted

the circular bubble sweater furiously in the evenings after work. I was not good at calculating gauge back then, and the sweater grew into something way too big. I kept going, determined to make it work, despite both the growing evidence to the contrary and the cat's fur working its way into the fuzzy orb.

Just as I was finishing the sweater, with barely enough yarn to finish the ribbed turtleneck collar, which actually truncated at my throat, my mother-in-law showed up for her annual visit. She admired my handiwork. When I tried the sweater on I looked like an aqua version of the girl who turns into the blueberry in *Willy Wonka and the Chocolate Factory*. It was the gauge, it was the drape. I should have adapted the pattern to a single strand of mohair for less bulk and wearability in the southern California climate. I should have made the longer, original version of the sweater to flatter my five-foot-nine height and small bones. I kept beating myself up about my mistakes. I could see the destiny of this sweater as my husband and I drove my mother-in-law around Los Angeles. The sweater was going to be ripped out, and I was going to ruin my first designer yarn purchase.

After my mother-in-law went back east, I spent the evenings ripping out the sweater. La Gran is Category Two: you can rip it out, but a devastating halo remains. I had hoped to re-ball the colors separately, but they were permanently entwined. So I reballed the double strands into eighteen balls, several of which the cat happily patted around the apartment. Surely I would be able to make something else with this yarn—a blanket for the cat, at least.

I read somewhere that if you wash unraveled mohair you can "bring it back." I tried washing a long length of double strand, and it returned to its haloed state, its original texture lost forever in my past.

My therapist at the time thought that my idea of ripping out and reusing the yarn was psychologically healthy. But months went by, and I didn't reuse the yarn. I finally decided that mohair is hot, and it sheds. I threw all eighteen balls into an old container in the corner of the bedroom. I stopped going to therapy.

My husband and I leased a house for a few years, and I made baby blankets for friends out of forgiving wool/acrylic blends. But our marriage was Category One: you can't rip it out without breaking. When the cat died and our landlord sold the house, we moved into another house and not two sweaters later I was moving into my own apartment with my growing stash of designer yarn, including the sad aqua mohair at the bottom of the oldest Rubbermaid container.

Around the time I filed for divorce, I poured myself some vodka and orange juice and stood in front of the spare bedroom closet, surveying the containers that made up my yarn stash. So many of the remnant balls recalled my marriage: two-ply merino for knitting socks on a trip to Napa, autumn-colored alpaca for a sweater I made to wear in the freezing meat-locker of an office in the old house. And there was the La Gran, never used for a blanket for my precious cat. My apartment was less than half the size of the houses where my husband and I had lived. And I was never going to use the yarn. I needed the space.

So I collected the eighteen balls and went to the kitchen pantry, a nice sized closet, one of the selling points for the apartment. I drank my vodka, and then I hurled the balls of La Gran one by one into the garbage can, each one making a definite thud more satisfying than the one before. I stopped at ball seventeen, the smallest ball, and I thought of the cat. I had loved the cat more than anything, maybe more than my husband. I put the final ball into one of the large plastic tubs at the back of my bedroom closet that contained the cat's stuff: toys, bowls, an acrylic blanket I had knitted him, and the clothes I had worn when we put him to sleep.

Then I took the garbage bag with the seventeen balls down to the carport and swung it into the Dumpster like a crazed anti-Santa. The garbage truck would come the next day, and those balls would be incinerated and turned into landfill, just as the cat's body had been a couple of years before.

They say you never really get divorced. There's always something: old tax returns with both of our names, emerald earrings he gave me before I left, memories of a beloved cat.

Some time later, I moved the eighteenth ball to my stash, knowing I would forget about it and rediscover it in years to come. Recently I started knitting a shawl with Colinette mohair purchased on eBay. I'm running out of yarn, and when I hunt through my stash I find the little ball of La Gran; it would work well with my color scheme. But I don't use it. It's a tiny orbital shrine to something tried, something failed, something I had to let go.

As for this new mohair, I suffer the greatest trepidation each time I pick up my needles, much like I experience on that rare first date that is going well. I am very, very careful with the stitches.

Something Precious for Lucy

Joanne Seiff

Last night I couldn't sleep. Outside, the gods played a summertime thunderstorm game of lawn bowls that lasted hours. Inside, the humid air hung stagnant around my husband's snores. I envied him his deep breaths, since my lungs felt burnt by ozone-induced asthma. I searched for a long-lost pattern in a knitting magazine. I tidied up my office. I crept downstairs for a comforting corn muffin snack and a glass of milk. Once downstairs, I gave in.

I sat down at my thirty-inch Canadian Production spinning wheel. I wanted to spin, but I didn't spin just what was convenient in the basket at hand. I didn't spin necessary yardage for a knitting project. No; insomnia spinning at one in the morning calls for something different. I got up again to look.

Several years ago, while I was in graduate school, I spun cast-off free fleeces from farmer friends. I still do this sometimes, but I did it then because of desperation. We didn't have the money to waste on anything extra. During that time, I saw an ad on the spinners' and weavers' housecleaning pages online. Someone came back from Asia with a lot of cashmere. They sold it raw for a fantastic price. I was thrilled with my discovery. I would wash it and card it. Of course I could dehair cashmere! It would be fine.

It was only after I won a ribbon at the North Carolina State Fair for my white, hand-knit, handspun cashmere lace scarf that I succumbed to the inevitable. My spinning and knitting may have won an award, but I found the scarf too itchy to wear. There were just a few more hairs left in that fiber. We were slightly better off financially when I sent the remainder of the fiber off to be dehaired.

I've moved twice since buying that fiber. The nearly perfect, dehaired three ounces of cashmere waited for a special project. I'd started spindling some of it once before, but with no project in mind, it felt wasteful. Now, at one in the morning, my reservations faded. I was desperate for calm. I was desperate for cool air in my lungs. I wished it would stop thundering. I wanted to be able to fall asleep. I took the cashmere in its supermarket plastic bag and headed toward my wheel.

My Canadian Production wheel sits in front of a church pew in our living room. Using a hand-knit pillow to prop myself forward, I began to spin. At first, I treadled quickly. The threadlike yarn sped through my fingers. Then I realized another reason why I couldn't sleep. I realized why I hadn't used this wheel in over a month.

A month ago my black dog died. She was special, as all dogs are to their owners, but Lucy was a bright border collie/lab mix who loved wool and spinners. When she died, I had to tell many spinners, because in North Carolina, New York, and Kentucky, she kept me company as I spun and knit. At guild meetings, Lucy would rest inside a circle of eight spinning wheels. She visited each spinner to smell their fiber, to receive affection, but she never distracted us from the task at hand. As I knit on the sofa, Lucy would curl close to me, warming my side. When I got this antique wheel in the winter of 2003, Lucy began a ritual. She sensed the calm of the slow treadling required for such a fast wheel. She always came to sit underneath me as I spun.

Last night, I stared out through a window into the stormy black backyard. Even though I couldn't see it in the dark, I looked out on Lucy's grave. Even so, I moved carefully. I felt Lucy's ghost below me, where she used to rest beneath the church pew and my feet. Lucy's body, once seventy-five pounds strong, wasted to forty some pounds during her struggle with liver cancer. We put her to sleep on June 7th, in our living room, when one of her lungs filled with fluid and she struggled to breathe.

Lucy hated thunderstorms. Perhaps now so do I. The lightning bolts felled trees all over our neighborhood last night. I was unable to sleep. Filled with adrenaline, I felt for something special to spin. I found cashmere, saved for years. Somehow, I knew one day I would need a comfort on a night like this. Slowly, slowly, my treadling slowed down. My breathing calmed. The ghost dog slept beneath my feet. The night quieted. At 2 A.M., I finally tired enough for sleep.

We spinners hoard and cherish fiber. I spin and knit whole fleeces' worth of coarse wool and pounds of roving during the day. Yet I savor the last bit of the fleece I bought on my honeymoon, or the rare breed Portland yarn I spun from fleece my husband bought me when we first started dating. I save bits of handspun yarn. I save the knitted roving mat I made to soak up Lucy's water bowl dribbles. Some fibers become precious when you need them to get through an emotional time. I didn't know until late last night that I needed that cashmere to get through a sleepless night and a long storm. I didn't know that the cashmere was for helping me to breathe. I didn't know it was for Lucy.

Carolyn's Creature Comforts

Karla Stover

On Vashon Island, Washington, a modest sign points down a narrow road leading the way to Creature Comforts, the cottage home and workplace of fiber artist Carolyn Smith. Carolyn's spinning wheel is in a glass-enclosed porch surrounded by masses of flowers. As she works she watches deer roam the valley on her land. Its rustic setting suits the dignity of its fifty-something owner, who is part of an effort to resurrect a local lost art.

One day in the 1960s, Carolyn stopped at the home of a good friend and Salish First Nation tribal member from Duncan, British Columbia, for a visit. Her friend had freshly washed dog fleece drying outside on a screen, and Carolyn expressed interest. One of the continuing legends of the Pacific Northwest's Salish people concerns their wool dogs—dogs whose hair was used to make clothing.

John Ledyard, who accompanied Captain James Cook on his exploration of the Pacific coast, mentioned the dogs in his writings, saying they were "almost white and of a domestic type." A more detailed description comes from the observations of Captain George Vancouver. In 1792, while anchored at Bainbridge Island, he wrote that the dogs resembled large Pomeranians. He described them as being shorn as sheep are in England. The Indian garments, he noted, were a combination of both coarse and fine wool and their abundance indicated easy access to the fleece.

The "Pomeranians" mentioned in Vancouver's journal were probably descendants of the large white Spitz dog from which the sled dogs of Iceland and Lapland, and the Chow, Husky, and Samoyed all evolved. To picture their presence among the Salish, whose territory extended from the Columbia River north into British Columbia, is no great stretch of the imagination.

In 1821, the arrival of the Hudson's Bay Company in the Pacific Northwest brought a change to the tradition. It became easier for the Indians to get blankets by bartering with the fur trading company than by making them. Dog hair weaving began to die out among the Salish, at least in practice if not in legend.

For Carolyn, the timeliness of the visit to her friend was a stroke of luck. The Salish woman taught her the skills of working with dog hair, and avocation soon became vocation.

"I decided that if I wanted to be a fiber artist then that's what I would be. I scavenged a little cabin and had it moved [to its present site], and went to work. As a natural fiber, dog hair is something hand spinners often use, but no one ever really made it known. In some European countries dog hair is regularly collected from grooming parlors and turned into textiles."

In an interview with the *Wall Street Journal*, Carolyn explained that "The process begins with combing, not clipping, your pet. Most dogs leave several sweaters worth of hair behind during the spring and fall shedding seasons. A brown paper bag full, about a pound, is generally enough."

Next she boils the fleece, adding borax to deodorize it.

When the fleece is dry she cards it with a small machine to remove short and undesirable fibers and to comb and make parallel those remaining. Because dogs don't perspire like sheep, their hair isn't as compatible with humans as wool is. So Carolyn blends dog hair and wool into a long strip, which she spins into yarn. Individuals can knit the yarn themselves or have Carolyn do it. When Carolyn does the knitting, she uses a knitting machine for the larger parts of the garment, but does all the small parts and finishing work by hand.

The finished product is lighter but warmer than wool and resembles angora in look and feel. The fleece is most attractive in its natural color, though Carolyn does occasionally dye the yarn.

All dog hair is not the same, and most fiber artists have a preference for the hair of a specific breed. Among the favorites are Bouvier, Poodle, Rottweiler, and Samoyed. The texture of Dalmatian and Staffordshire Bull Terrier hair makes it unsuitable.

There is no dog hair apparel trade association, but professional weavers say business and interest is up. The popularity of using Fido's hair in garments is catching on. Carolyn's first step in starting her business was to run an ad in *Dog Fancy* magazine: "Hand spinner makes sweaters, blankets, yarn, or other articles from your dog's hair." Though not overwhelming, the response was swift.

Carolyn is one of many people nationwide whose fascination with the colors and textures of a variety of natural fibers is not limited to the obvious. "I just got back from a trip to New Zealand where possum hair is being made into sweaters, gloves and hats," she says.

Like all artists, she likes to experiment. She has tried horse, cat, llama, rabbit, and even human hair. Chinchilla combings, she discovered, make a wonderful garment without having to kill the animal. There is a wolf preserve near her home, and Carolyn has worked with their hair too. Currently, she is arranging for a shipment of silver fox hair from a Montana breeder, and while waiting is experimenting with cat hair. "Cat hair makes wonderful felt," she says, "and the felt makes great vests—wearable art."

The choice of fiber is, after all, only limited by imagination.

Problem Skeins

Rusty Haskell

Trying to liquidate some portion of my yarn supply, I have picked up one of my problem skeins. Every knitter knows about problem skeins. These are the balls of yarn that you bought for reasons so nebulous that they shouldn't even be considered reasons. Sometimes you find a sale and pick up several skeins in a mad flurry of consumerism. Sometimes you fall in love with a particular color and find that it mysteriously follows you home with only a charge to your credit card as forensic evidence.

In my case, the problem skein I picked up out of my stash is a ball of Lion Brand Chenille Thick and Quick in a color that can only be called Cookie Monster blue. I bought this yarn because the blue is so bright that it has a sort of halo of blueness about it. This yarn belongs in the realm of Platonic ideals as the prime example of what the color blue is—what blue should aspire to be in our imperfect realm of shadows. I bought the yarn right after I started knitting because it seemed a damned sight more interesting than my little acrylic garter swatches. Not understanding the cruel dictates of dye lots and yarn color variation, I bought only one skein of this muppetesque yarn.

I hit the Internet to find some sort of muse to inspire me. I had to find some way of ridding my stash of a ball of yarn that has been nagging me, begging for its own special purpose for nearly two months. I quickly found that there is little that I care to do with a lone skein of yarn as bulky as this. Socks are out of the question. I can't seem to find a pair of double-pointed needles in size 10 anywhere in the immediate area, which rules the possibility of a hat out as well. I researched charities to which I might donate something useful. I looked at stuffed animal patterns and afghans. Everything I found to do with this yarn required the purchase either of more (equally bulky) yarn or of needles to work this elephantine cord.

This is crux of my dilemma, you see. Yarn, for knitters, is our creative medium. We tend to be inspired by fiber. Upon finding that perfect variety of yarn at a local yarn store, it's like the projects create themselves. Why, this wool would be perfect for an Aran sweater! This mohair would make an awesome hat. In a fit of inspiration and needlework horniness, we whip out whatever means of payment happens to be convenient and purchase all the hardware and incidentals required to realize our creative vision.

But no such thing happens with the problem skein. The idea of buying needles and notions to actually work the dreaded fiber is itself anathema. The Cookie Monster yarn gets passed over because it's way bulkier than anything else in my stash. I have a bias against bulky knits, to be honest, and therefore I lack the needles necessary to work anything that bills itself as "Thick and Quick." I tend to consider things knitted on size 7 needles to be just about as bulky as I can take.

But of course I had to get rid of this yarn in some fashion. Accompanying my wife Allyson to the local Michael's, the Wal-Mart of crafts, I ended up purchasing a pair of straight aluminum size 10 needles and steeled my resolve to actually *do* something with this damnable yarn. When I got home, I decided to cast on before my resolve lessened and I put Cookie Monster back in the yarn box. Casting on as many of the mammoth stitches as I could possibly fit on my needles, I decided that the size most closely resembled the dimensions of a couch throw pillow. A blue throw pillow that looks more at home on Sesame Street than on my non-existent couch. It would do.

The yarn knit up as quickly as billed, and for that, I'm thankful. I'm making plans for which victim—charity or family member—will inherit my stash-reducing pillow, but I have this terrible fear that the pillow will remain in my house like some kind of cursed object created to haunt my offspring for generations to come. Perhaps, however, it will perform a valuable service as a reminder that I shouldn't buy yarn I have no immediate use for. Perhaps it will encourage me to flirt with yarn, as Allyson does: visiting the yarn supplier, caressing the yarn, giving the skein that come-hither look with a coquettish twist of the head, dreaming of what wonderful project this fiber might inspire—until the day comes when the knitting lust can no longer be bottled up and the yarn gets snatched up in a torrid flash of carnal consumerism.

Or maybe I should just buy a bigger plastic container for my stash.

The Art of Poverty

Suzanne M. Cody

Back in the days when dinosaurs roamed the earth, my mother used to take sweaters from the Salvation Army Free Box, unravel them and re-knit the yarn into things she hoped my sister, my brother, and I might consent to wear. Whether or not we ever wore these things is up for debate. The issue wasn't as much wearing something someone else had already worn, but wearing something *remade* from something someone else had already worn to the point that the Salvation Army wouldn't even sell it. Now *that's* poverty.

My mother's hands were constantly busy. She sewed, knit, embroidered, painted, stenciled, built; she created and re-created. I, on the other hand, was more interested in the creative life of the *mind.* I knew the basics of knitting, sewing, what-have-you, but I was going to be a writer, an actress, a musician—I was going to be an *artist,* by God, not a mere craftsperson. Sure, the things my mother made were kind of cool, but I was all about *art,* not utilitarian objects.

Twenty years later, see how the mighty have fallen.

Or have they?

As a matter of fact, I didn't become an actress, a musician, or much of a writer. Instead, I moved to the Midwest, found a job at a bookstore, and had a beautiful accidental baby. I left my dreams of art behind to take on the day-to-day business of raising a child on my own, getting us through financially and emotionally.

Several non-knitting years later, I moved in with J. He was a sweet man who understood the importance of financial stability, especially to a scrabbling single mother. As a builder and worker with his hands, he was also a staunch advocate of using the right tools and materials for every job. When I decided I was going to pick up knitting again, he insisted that I have the proper tools (I am the proud owner of many lovely bamboo and birch needles), as well as a fine supply of good quality yarns. He became the enabler of my burgeoning fiber addiction ("Well, at least it's not crack," he would say when as I hauled in another bagful). No Salvation Army Rejects for me!

Eventually, though, J. left, taking financial stability with him. I sent my daughter to kindergarten, went to work full time, took over paying the rent and bills and subsequently entered the deepest throes of fiber withdrawal. Though not to the point where I was scavenging Dumpsters for returnables, I certainly couldn't take my weekly jaunt to the yarn store. My steady supply of Brown Sheep had dried up. No more Koigu, no more Tahki/Stacy Charles, GGH, Cascade, Mountain Colors—you name it and I couldn't have it. I put down my needles in despair.

Then one day, as my daughter rummaged through an overfull closet, she popped open a tote and pulled out—a ball of yarn. "Mama?" she said, turning the fluffy pink ball over in her hands, "Could you make me something out of this?" She dropped it on the floor and pulled out another ball, equally fluffy, but sherbet orange. "Out of this, too!" She tugged at the tote until it came out of the closet, and there underneath it was another tote, and another, and another, *all full of yarn.*

It was my Thrift Store Stash.

The Thrift Store Stash had accumulated through my compulsive need to buy yarn paired with my compulsive need to thrift shop. Our local Mennonite-run shop was a treasure trove of old, funky, and discontinued (*long* discontinued) yarns. They were so damn cheap, I never could bring myself to leave them there. In all, I had eight totes of yarn, as well as several plastic grocery bags. "Look at this!" my daughter said, holding up a ball of Yarns Brunswick Eleganza (even the names of these yarns were dated). She found a skein of something called Berroco Dji Dji ("an unusual Irish import brushed variegated yarn in three colors") and some Phildar Broadway, all mohairy and sparkly.

There were so many colors and textures, so much variety, my hands just itched to pick up some needles and have at it. But what to do? My problem was I had been pattern-bound for so long I didn't have the first real idea how to go about it on my own. My mother's voice echoed in the back of my brain: "Waste not, want not," she said.

So I started to swatch. Just to see how things looked at this gauge or that gauge, how they draped, how they felt against my skin, how they stretched, or didn't. I compared my gauges to patterns I had in books and thought about tweaking a bit here and there to accommodate what I had available. I took books of stitch patterns out of the library and knit up lace scarves out of anything I had fewer than two balls of. I figured out the mathematics of hats and mittens. I kept a calculator in my knitting bag at all times, as well as a cloth tape measure for impromptu measuring sessions.

Soon I was seeing everything cozied—telephone cozies, chair cozies, shoe cozies, computer monitor cozies. Every three-dimensional thing I imagined covered in something warm and soft. I thought about knitting *in* three dimensions, not just teddy bears and stuffed bunnies, but odd-shaped creatures that might reflect what I was feeling inside a lot of the time—kind of out of place, distorted and unformed. I held skeins and balls of all types up against each other, envisioning them knitted together in various ways and hung in copper wire frames. It was an epiphany. Suddenly, yarn was more than a potential sweater or mitten or scarf; it was a *medium*. And with a medium, a few tools and my imagination in overdrive I could make *anything*.

No, I am not the first person to think like this. I realize now that there are artists who create incredible, inspired sculptures with (something like) two sticks and (the general idea of) string. But until I came to it on my own (or, more accurately, poverty dragged me there, kicking and screaming), I didn't even know that they were out there, doing these amazing things. Have you heard about the woman who crochets sushi?

But it is not the odd shapes and non-standard materials that make craft into art, I think. It is the effort and the emotion that goes into the piece, what the maker is trying to convey. If it is love, or warmth, or affection, is that not as artistic as something less easily accessible to the observer? If I knit a beautiful sweater of my own design out of found materials for someone I love, is that less of a work of art than a wall hanging or a computer monitor cozy or a giant sock?

I often hear actors refer to acting as "my craft." I think I will, from now on, refer to my knitting as "my art." Look, Mom. I *am* an artist.

Why God Gave Us a Sense of Humor

Anne McKee

If I'd pawed a little more vigorously though the box, I would have discovered them. But I saw the laceweight alpaca on top, was seduced, and bid for the lot. It was only when I got the box home from the Complete Contents Auction Sale that I found them—an assortment of freakishly colored, petroleum-based skeins of knitting product buried at the bottom of the container. I'm sure you've seen them, in bargain basements, bagged at the Sally Ann, and at yard sales. And you've probably wondered, as I did, where on earth this stuff comes from. After some consideration, I've come up with a plausible scenario.

I suggest that someone still reeling from a longstanding illness purchased these bizarre bargains at the sale table of a knitting shop. The skeins had been sent to the knitting shop as a "bonus" for purchasing the most wool product that past August. They stayed in that bargain shopper's overstuffed closets until she was well, at which point she promptly weeded her stash. From there the skeins went to a rummage sale where they were foisted upon some unsuspecting soul who found them in the bottom of a bag lot for which she'd paid a dollar. When she died, her relatives shoved them into the bottom of a box and cleverly positioned alpaca laceweight on top. Which brings them to me. I will probably send this product—whose extraordinary colors would stun a Crayola color engineer—to the dump, where it will sit for eternity, scaring rats.

As I stare at this product, I imagine how much must have gone into the creation of something so vile:

Millions and millions of years ago, in a time we humans have chosen to call the Paleozoic, much of the present land masses were covered by warm salt-water seas. In these seas swam all manner of creatures. As they died, they sank to the bottom of the seas and rotted. Over time these dead things were shaped by heat and pressure into deposits of oil, gas, and coal. They sat undiscovered until . . . somebody's little girl decided that geology would make an excellent career choice. The child went to school, studied with diligence, partied conservatively, and graduated with a degree which she proudly displayed at the recruiting table at an oil and gas expo. Next stop—a desk covered with drill logs and maps.

After much careful study, the peon geologist placed, with a tremulous hand (drilling is a very expensive thing to do), an X on the spot she felt would yield oil. The X was placed on the desks of more senior geologists, who passed it yet higher on the chain of command until that X was stamped and approved, finally due to become a hole.

Crews went out and cleared the site of trees and shrubs and grasses, scaring away all living things, built roads and brought in the rig. It was carefully placed on the X. The peon geologist was allowed to go up to the site to stand alongside the senior site geologist and watch the core as it came out of the hole. She was thrilled and scared. Would it be dry? Would failure besmirch her career?

It was not dry. Oil flowed.

After a myriad of tests by petroleum engineers, the data was passed to economists who determined that enough oil flowed to make the hole economically viable. "Yeah!" said the peon geologist and went back to her maps and drill logs, determined to find another prosperous X.

Meanwhile . . .

The oil was gathered from the hole and sent to a refinery. From there it flowed along a pipeline to a holding tank at the edge of a major body of water. A ship came in and the oil was pumped aboard. Once the ship was full a pilot came on board and directed the captain how to get to sea. Once he disembarked, the captain sat on the bridge and enjoyed the vista until land was sighted, thousands of miles from the geologist's X.

The ship was berthed, and the oil pumped to dockside tanks. From there it was pumped into a tanker-trailer driven by a man whose wife was unhappy because he'd been on the road far too much. He delivered it to a factory run by a man who had been told that knitting was again becoming very popular. He studied the economics, rejigged the machinery, and used that oil to make petroleum-based knitting product. Unfortunately, he was both bilious and color-blind. Furthermore, he was involved in a major feud with his product engineer involving gambling debts and scurrilous expense submissions. The color choice was the product engineer's revenge. The product eventually created—enough to fill several shipboard containers—the factory manager sent to market half a world away because he did not want it known in his own country that he'd squandered a non-renewable resource creating something *this* horrible. His receivers eyed it with horror and sent it as a "bonus" to shops that had made large orders.

I have always envisioned that when I die, my bits and pieces will fertilize a wheat field or a roadside bank of wildflowers. There is, however, a chance that millions and millions of years from now my bits and pieces will end up used to create a product that isn't even wanted at a Complete Contents Auction Sale.

Thank you, God, for a giving us a sense of humor.

About Our Authors and Editors

JUDITH ADER lives in California with her two favorite guys—her husband and her son. Currently she works for a defense company, developing databases and writing procedures. She has a psychology degree, has traveled extensively, and loves to go camping. She knits to relax and writes to feed her soul.

PENELOPE ALLEN is a gainfully employed Canadian author who resides in Vancouver, British Columbia. Serendipity inspired her to begin writing poetry in 1998 but she's been knitting since she was eight. While raising her son, Kevin, she was also active in her union and is an ardent supporter of the labor movement.

ROBIN M. ALLEN is a writer, reader, knitter, Scrabbler, and raw vegan. She lives in a little red house in south Texas, where there is no need for the sweaters she doesn't finish.

LILLY ALLISON lives and attempts to knit in Irving, Texas, where she works as a freelance writer. She and her husband, Don, have two children, three dogs, and a cat. Her current knitting challenge is a doggie sweater for a dachshund. She can be reached at lattelal@yahoo.com.

JEANNINE BAKRIGES is an exuberant fiber arts instructor and practitioner living in Whitingham, Vermont. She's been known to tell students that she's often experienced a strong, primordial desire to roll and revel in a superbly clean and glistening, grease-free sheep's fleece.

MAGGIE CALVIN, a native of Iowa, now lives in Maine, with her building-contractor husband and two kids. She is a devoted socko-holic and part-time teacher.

ELLIOTT CARPENITO lives in Waban, Massachusetts, with his husband, Tony, and their son, Michael. A maniacal knitter, Elliott can be seen knitting at any time, in any place. Perhaps someday he will be able to fulfill his fantasy of owning a yarn store café on the water.

KATIE CHILTON, who lives in Joliet, Illinois, taught herself to knit many years ago. She works as a middle-school librarian, and recently completed an MFA in writing from the Stonecoast program in Maine—one reason her husband is still waiting for the brown alpaca vest that inspired her poem.

CHARMIAN CHRISTIE is a writer living in Guelph, Ontario, where the cold weather enables her knitting addiction. Her work has been heard on CBC national radio and appears in various magazines and anthologies, including *KnitLit (too)*. Feel free to sample her writing at www.mybrainchild.biz/.

LORRAINE LENER CIANCIO, writer and knitter, has just discovered digital photography. Her essays and poetry have been published in anthologies and reviews. She was editor of *Chokecherries* anthology for seven years and quit to devote more time to travel, writing, knitting, and photography. She lives at 7,500 feet in Taos, New Mexico.

E. B. CLUTTER lives in Toronto, Ontario, and spends much of her time reading and writing. She is grateful to the knitters in her life for their bounteous gifts, among these her late mother Annie, her friend Judi, and her daughter Gillian, whose finely knit jewelry in gold and silver wire is a joy to behold. Clutter's story "The Artist" appeared in *KnitLit (too)*.

SUZANNE CODY has written about knitting in *KnitLit (too)*, as well as in *The Knitter's Gift* (Adams Media, 2004). She knits, writes, and raises her daughter in Iowa City, Iowa.

KARNA CONVERSE writes from her home in Storm Lake, Iowa, where she lives with her husband and their three children. She knits while she waits: for kids to get out of school, for kids to practice music and sports, and for kids after they've been out with friends.

CATHY COOPER is a native New Yorker living in Greenwich Village with her husband, daughter, and two cats. By day, she manages customer analysis as a senior vice president at the leading marketing communications agency, Wunderman. By night (on airplanes or buses, in coffee shops and taxis), she crochets and knits.

FRAN CORRIVEAU resides in Northampton, Massachusetts, with her long-term partner and their eight rabbits. She enjoys singing jazz, hiking the forest trails of New England, and long beach walks on the coast of Maine. Her knitting remains marginal but nevertheless enjoyable. Her mother, the real knitter, is eighty-eight and enjoying life as it comes with an amazing attitude.

MARYLOU DIPIETRO is a poet, playwright, and artist, working in mosaics and fibers. Her poems have been published in numerous literary magazines and her plays have been produced in the Boston area. She has a passion for antiques, so when she and her husband bought an 1850 farmhouse in southern New Hampshire, she opened an antique shop in the barn (www.cheshamdepotantiques.com).

PAULA E. DREW was born in England. She teaches foreign languages. She enjoys the friendship and artistic inspiration of being a member of Jersey Knitters. She loves to roller-skate, read, and perform in community theater. She lives in Randolph, New Jersey, with her husband, Ben.

Knitting and storytelling are two of **KATE DUDDING**'s passions. Since 1963, Kate has been knitting and designing sweaters. Since 1989, she has been telling stories to audiences at venues in the northeastern USA. One of her stories was published in *KnitLit (too)*. See her website for other stories: www.katedudding.com.

JENNY FELDON is an MFA candidate in fiction at the New School University. When she's not writing, reading, or knitting, Jenny can be found teaching and practicing yoga, spending time with family and friends, and trying to live the best life she possibly can. She lives in Manhattan with her husband, Jay, and their small white dog, Tucker.

MARJORIE FLATHERS has been a freelance writer for twenty-five years and a knitter for twice that long. Her work has been in print over 300 times, and her children's stories appear regularly in the *Los Angeles Times*. Married for forty-four years, she has three grown children and five grandchildren and has lived most of her life in San Bernardino, California.

KAY FLORES lives in Casper, Wyoming, in a home that is blessedly free of rodents. Kay spends many happy hours knitting so that her children, grandchildren, and friends will have warm, woolly socks. She is active in the Episcopal church and in her spare time works for the Wyoming Department of Employment.

BARBARA FORNOFF is a social worker and a native of Alexandria, Virginia. She remembers being mesmerized by the feeling of cloth at a young age. Learning to weave and knit unraveled the source of her fascination: she wanted to know how to create fabric! Barbara enjoys mastering all the design elements of textiles.

JENNY FROST learned to knit from her grandmother when she was seven and has been at it with varying degrees of intensity ever since. The number of decades covered during this time is alarming. She has a very tolerant husband and the three best children in the world—all of whom know to ask first if she's counting before speaking. She works in publishing in Manhattan.

TZIVIA GOVER's poems have appeared in dozens of periodicals and anthologies including *Lilith, The Bark*, and *Grrrrr: A Collection of Poems About Bears*. She is the author of *Mindful Moments for Stressful Days* (Storey, 2002). She received her MFA in writing from Columbia University and teaches poetry to teen mothers in Holyoke, Massachusetts.

RUSTY HASKELL is a computer programmer at the University of Florida registrar's office. He lives in Gainesville with his wife, Allyson, and enjoys punk rock, dark-roasted coffee, and Unix-based operating systems. Rusty is the site administrator and chief contributor to Bactroid.net, turning free time into something suspiciously like work.

SUSANNA HEATH lives in northwestern Massachusetts with her husband, three young children, and two Shelties, Max and Morag. She aspires to be a writer, if she can ever find her desk—it's under there somewhere. . . .

MARTHA HESSELEIN lives in Mobile, Alabama, with her wonderful husband, amazing daughter, and a bewildering assortment of pets. She works as a management consultant, Web designer, and part owner of The YarnHaus (www.yarnhaus.com), a fabulous LYS. She gratefully celebrated her first year free from cancer in November 2004.

ANN HOOD is the author of seven novels, including *Somewhere off the Coast of Maine, Ruby: A Memoir, Do Not Go Gentle, My Search for Miracles in a Cynical Time*, and *An Ornithologist's Guide to Life*, a collection of short stories. She lives and knits in Providence, Rhode Island, where she has just completed a new novel, *The Knitting Circle*.

SANDRA HURTES is a writer living in New York. Her articles and essays have appeared in *The New York Times, The Washington Post, Poets & Writers*, and numerous other publications. Before leaving her knitting needles behind, her sweater patterns appeared in *Family Circle* and *McCall's Needlework & Crafts*.

ALISON JEPPSON HYDE is a writer who returned to knitting passionately when her children were small: it stays done, she loves creating something beautiful, it lets her give freely of the best in herself, and she considers knitting to be time and love made tangible. Her website is www.spindyeknit.com.

JENNIFER JAMESON is a technical writer who lives in Los Angeles. Her spare time is mainly consumed by salsa dancing and organizing her yarn stash. She also teaches a knitting class at Wildfiber in Santa Monica. Her essay about knitting and dating was published last year in *The Knitter's Gift*.

MARIA JERINIC knits and lives in Henderson, Nevada, with her husband (another Bond fan) and three children. She serves as an editor for *Topics for Victorian Literature and Culture* and teaches English part-time at UNLV. She recently completed a cardigan for her toddler daughter, who refuses to wear it.

BETTY JONES lives south of Atlanta amidst a clutter of cats, spinning wheels, looms, and antique sewing machines. She belongs to Peachtree Handspinners Guild and to Treadle On, a group promoting the use of people-powered sewing machines. A self-proclaimed "hack of all trades but master of none," she believes there is always something new (or old) to learn.

HARRY KELLEY shepherded with his husband, James Londagin, until James's death in a farm accident in December 2004. Claire Londagin, for whom the expressive Ninotchka's bell tolls, is James's and Harry's niece. The poem was written to accompany the sweater, which indeed is brown-and-white striped with bright rainbow accents.

CANDACE KEY has the good fortune to live, work, and knit in the San Francisco area, where she fantasizes about a day when she will have more time to knit, write, and finally develop all those designs in her head.

GRAZYNA J. KOZACZKA has received her Ph.D. in American literature from the Jagiellonian University in Krakow, Poland, and currently teaches English at Cazenovia College in Cazenovia, New York. Among other publications, she is the author of *Old World Stitchery for Today*, a book devoted to traditional Polish needlework techniques.

SUSAN WEST KURZ is the president of Dr. Hauschka Skin Care, Inc., and the author of *Healing Beauty the Dr. Hauschka Way*, available in April 2006. She began knitting late in life after she and her husband adopted two children from Guatemala. A perfect day for Susan includes Dr. Hauschka Rose Cream, Mostly Merino yarns, and a good story.

JULIA LASALLE is an aspiring knitter with two hats, several scarves, and one atrociously misshapen circus-clown sweater to her credit. She is a graduate of Carnegie Mellon and Duquesne University in Pittsburgh, Pennsylvania.

MINDY LEARY has lived in Anchorage, Alaska, since 1962. As a bookkeeper and B&B owner, her duties are divided between operation of the two family businesses, Boot Country and the Snoozin' Moose Inn. Spare time is spent knitting in the comfy leather chair by the fireplace, with tabby cat Lucille on her lap.

MARSHA LETOURNEAU is a longtime fiberist and sometime word weaver whose work has appeared in fiber newsletters and *Spin Off*. She lives in Maine with a fiber-equipment business and an indulgent husband. They love old things and old ways—also books, hikes, water and snow sports, and being grandparents.

Textiles have been **DIANNE LITTLE**'s avocation and vocation. She has been working in textiles for over fifty years as a spinner, knitter, quilter, rug hooker, weaver, and embroiderer. Through education her avocation became a vocation as a textile specialist/conservator. Dianne's last employment before retiring was that of textile conservator for RMS *Titanic* artifacts.

SUSAN GORDON LYDON is the author of *Knitting Heaven and Earth: Healing the Heart with Craft*, as well as *The Knitting Sutra* and

Take the Long Way Home. She has been writing professionally and knitting passionately for more than forty years. She lives in the San Francisco Bay area.

SAMANTHA LYNN is a Chicago-based writer currently trying to sell her first novel and working on a second between the knitting projects. In the fall of 2004 she managed to knit up the bulk of her excess stash, and the cat continues in robust health. She blogs her adventures at www.livejournal.com/users/robling_t.

MICHELLE MACH is a librarian in Colorado. Her essays and short stories have appeared in several magazines and anthologies, including *ByLine Magazine* and *Simple Pleasures of Friendship (2004)*. She fervently hopes that Neal will resume knitting one day.

CHERYL MANDALA first picked up knitting needles in April 2004 and hasn't put them down since. When not knitting, spinning, or writing about knitting and spinning, Cheryl practices law in the San Francisco Bay Area, where she lives with her husband, Terry and her spinning wheel, Suzie. You can read her blog at www.purlinterrupted.com/.

ADRIENNE MARTINI has been a theater technician, apprentice massage therapist, bookstore bookkeeper, and a pizza joint waitress. Currently, she is working on a memoir called *Hillbilly Gothic*, to be published by The Free Press in 2006. Maddy is now three and has a sibling on the way.

JENNIFER MCCANN is a stay-at-home mom who lives with her husband and son in eastern Washington State. She spends her time parenting, cooking, reading, knitting, and blogging all about it at shmooblog.blogspot.com/. She is currently learning lace knitting and has embarked on her first Norwegian sweater.

JANE MCDERMOTT lives, writes, loves, runs, plays the ukulele and accordion, grows vegetables and olives, raises bees, hopes to raise chickens, basks in the glamour of marketing for a legal publisher but, alas, does not knit in Oakland, California. Some things are best left to others.

ANNE MCKEE was raised on the Canadian prairies. She is a geologist by trade and has knocked rocks from one end of northern Canada to the other. Since there is as much fantasy in science as there is in fiction, her decision to switch from report writing to fiction writing wasn't difficult. She currently lives with her family in Oakville, Ontario.

Artist, writer, spinner, knit designer, and recovering lawyer, **NILDA MESA** learned knitting from her Spanish grandmother. Her work appeared in *Knit Lit (too)* and *Stitch 'n Bitch Nation*. She has exhibited in New York and France. She and her husband, Robert Seyffert, run a summer artist residency program in Brittany, France. The rest of the year they live in Harlem with their two kids and two cats. See more at nildamesa.typepad.com/waltzing_knitilda.

COREY MESLER has published in numerous journals and anthologies. His novel *Talk: A Novel in Dialogue* was released in 2002. He also has a number of poetry chapbooks available. In 2005 his second novel, *We Are Billion-Year-Old Carbon*, will be released. With his wife, he runs Burke's Book Store in Memphis, Tennessee.

BRIGITTE MINER considers knitting to be as thrilling as other adventures she pursues, among them cob house making, home-schooling her daughter, swimming butterfly upstream, and meditating. While many people mistake her sister Karen's knitted masterpieces as being machine made, no one mistakes Brigitte's work to be anything other than homemade. She can be reached at allinnerpeace@yahoo.com.

CINDY MONTE knits, quilts, and sews in Seattle with grade schoolers, her own boys (ages seven and three), and on very rare occasions, her husband, Kevin, who believes that if criminals were forced to do handwork, they would never return to prison. In spite of this, she's been loving him for more than twenty-five years.

CHERYL MURRAY knits for her husband, Rick, and her daughter, Cara, in Kansas City. A microbiologist by training, she never thought of herself as artistic until she discovered yarn. She currently teaches anywhere they'll let her in an effort to meet a personal goal of teaching the entire world to knit.

PEGGY NEUBER comes from a long line of women who find pleasure in handwork, so it was natural for her never to have idle hands even as a child. Now, as an adult, knitting is the best way she knows to lower blood pressure. She lives in Logan, Utah with her family and two cats who love to hide yarn all over the house.

DOROTHY NORTH, a poet and writer, lives near San Francisco, where she practices law. Her work has appeared in *Poet Lore*, *Hotel Amerika*, and *I Thought My Father Was God*, the anthology edited by Paul Auster. In addition to being a lifelong knitter, she has won numerous ribbons for her quilting. She is a graduate of Barnard College, New York City, and Hastings College of Law, San Francisco.

STEPHANIE PEARL-MCPHEE lives in Toronto with her three daughters and a wool-sympathetic spouse. She is the author of *At Knit's End: Meditations for Women Who Knit Too Much* and *Yarn Harlot: The Secret Life of a Knitter*. She blogs about wool, knitting, and the meaning of life and laundry at www.yarnharlot.ca.

NORAH PIEHL's essays and articles have appeared in the anthology *The Knitter's Gift*, *Pregnancy* magazine, and other publications. She is a regular book reviewer for *Brain, Child*, and *The Horn Book Guide*. Norah is an editor and permissions researcher who lives outside Boston with her husband, her two-year-old son, and way too much yarn.

SUSAN BLACKWELL RAMSEY is a bookseller at the only bookstore in town older than she is. She also teaches women's literature at Kalamazoo College's Stryker Center, as well as handspinning and knitting (it's a small town) at the Kalamazoo Institute of Arts.

DEBORAH ROBSON learned to knit, purl, and cast on while sitting on a loveseat next to her grandmother and became an avid knitter when she went to college. She lives in Colorado with her daughter, two dogs, and a cat. They all work together in a small publishing company named Nomad Press.

LINDA ROGHAAR, a Massachusetts native, has deep ties (yarn and otherwise) to Maine, New Hampshire, and Vermont. With her family (including the amazing golden retriever, Ellie), she continues to be surprised at how knitting affects her life. She is a literary agent in Amherst, Massachusetts.

A newcomer to the craft of knitting, **AMY ROSENSTEIN** hopes someday to construct something slightly more complex than an uneven two-foot-long scarf. Until then, project recipients, beloved hubby David and toddler Jakob, should just grin and wear it!

After Chicago, Atlanta, and Phoenix, **L. S. ROWE** is happy in the village of Grass Lake, Michigan, where her three small children can play with neighborhood kids and walk to school. Lisa spins, weaves, writes fiction, and is trying to become a knitwear designer—one place her education (architecture) and passion (knitting) intersect.

JOANNE SEIFF is a writer and educator. Her fiber-related writing is on Knitty.com and in *Spin-Off* and *Wild Fibers* magazines. The Kentucky Foundation for Women recently awarded Joanne a grant to write an essay collection, *Knitting Is Good for You*, about knitting as it affects intellectual growth and health.

ANN SHAYNE is the coauthor, with Kay Gardiner, of *Mason-Dixon Knitting*, a book to be published in spring 2006 by Clarkson Potter Publishers. Ann and Kay carry on pretty much every day at www.masondixonknitting.com.

In addition to a full time job, **KARLA STOVER** writes two monthly newspaper columns: one on Pacific Northwest history and one on day trips to small towns. She also has a weekly radio spot, talking about the early years on Puget Sound. "There probably has never been anything that I can't find some interest in," she says, "including fiber art."

LAURAN STRAIT, a freelance writer and professional editor, teaches writing and editing, and facilitates several year-round writers' workshops. She edits for *Moondance Magazine*, an international woman's e-zine, and for *NFG*, a Canadian print magazine. Her work has been published in numerous print and online magazine and literary reviews, and she has won the occasional writing contest. Contact the author at laurans@hotmail.com.

KATHRYN TEWSON is thirty years old and lives in Seattle with the love of her life. She knits, crochets, hand-dyes yarn and textiles, spins, and sings, although usually not all at once. She is the president and cofounder of Made With Love by a Liberal; see www.madewithlovebyaliberal.org.

Since writing this essay, **AMY E. TYLER** has moved from Nebraska to where her soul resides: the northwest corner of the Lower Peninsula of Michigan, near Interlochen. There she knits and spins, designs and teaches.

MARILYN WEBSTER currently makes her home in Sonoma County, California, and works for Alchemy Yarns of Transformation.

MARGARET KLEIN WILSON is the owner of Mostly Merino, a fiber studio specializing in hand-dyed luxury yarns, knitting kits, and custom-knit sweaters. Margaret is the author and editor of *The Green Mountain Spinnery Knitting Book*. Her writing has also appeared in *Interweave Knits*, *Handwoven*, and *Knit Lit: Sweaters and Their Stories*. A shepherd, dyer, and designer, she writes and keeps sheep in Dummerston, Vermont.

MOLLY WOLF is the author of *Hiding in Plain Sight*, *A Place Like Any Other*, *Angels and Dragons*, and *White China*, all books about finding God in everyday life. She co-edits the *KnitLit* series with Linda Roghaar. She lives in Kingston, Ontario, with her two grown sons, her knitting daughter, and three cats. See her website, sabbathblessings.org and her spinning blog, spindlegeek@blog–aty.com.

MARGE WOOLEY now calls New Hampshire her final stop after growing up in New Jersey then living in Colorado for twenty-six years. Her passions include golf, knitting, and the Siberian huskies that she has loved and been loved by over the last thirty-five years.

Dear Reader:

Thanks so much for spending time with our friends and us. Don't forget to visit our website, www.knitlit.com, which gives you information about the other two *KnitLit* books. It provides information on our contributors, charity knitting, and knit-ins. It gives links to fascinating fiber sites. We're thinking about new, neat additions to the site, so do keep dropping in! We'll keep you abreast of plans for new books. And we love to get your feedback.

May your skeins stay untangled and your gauges correct, and may your double-pointed needles never, ever vanish under the sofa.

All the best—
Linda and Molly

CELEBRATE THE JOY OF KNITTING WITH <u>KNITLIT</u>!

Read the first two books in the KnitLit series—
packed full of hilarious essays,
inspiring anecdotes, and touching recollections
from knitters all over the globe.

KnitLit
0-609-80824-9
$13.00 paper
(Canada: $20.00)

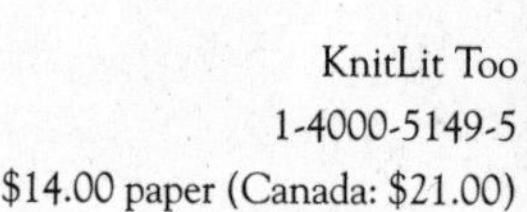

KnitLit Too
1-4000-5149-5
$14.00 paper (Canada: $21.00)

THREE RIVERS PRESS • NEW YORK
Available wherever books are sold
www.threeriverspress.com